Cognitive Footprints:

Tracing Human Nature Through Psychology

Cognitive Footprints: Tracing Human Nature Through Psychology

Published By: Wissira Research Lab LLC

Imprint Name: Wissira Press

US Office: Carmel, United States- 46074

India Office: KDP, RNE, India-201017

Email: editor@wissira.us, **Website:** https://books.wissira.us

Mobile: +91 7535 916 555

Prof. Dr. Anu Kant Mital

ISBN - 978-93-7559-837-4

Maharaja Agrasen Himalayan Garhwal University,

Address: Uttarakhand, India

Edition: 2026

Printed In: India

Maharaja Agrasen Himalayan Garhwal University,

Address: Uttarakhand, India

Cognitive Footprints:

Tracing Human Nature Through Psychology

2026

Authors:

Prof. Dr. Anu Kant Mital

Published By

Wissira Research Lab

ISBN 978-93-7559-837-4

9 789375 598374

Preface

The field of cognitive psychology has long been a cornerstone of understanding human nature, offering profound insights into how we think, learn, remember, and interact with the world. ***Cognitive Footprints: Tracing Human Nature Through Psychology*** seeks to illuminate the intricate workings of the human mind through the lens of cognitive processes, examining how mental functions shape our perceptions, decisions, emotions, and social interactions. In this book, we embark on a journey through the foundational theories, current research, and future directions in the realm of cognitive psychology.

The aim of this book is not only to explore the cognitive mechanisms that drive human behaviour but also to understand the way these mechanisms evolve and adapt over time, in response to both internal and external influences. From the intricacies of memory and decision-making to the profound impact of emotions on cognition, we will explore how human cognition is intertwined with our social environment, mental health, and technological advancements.

Each chapter delves into a unique aspect of cognitive psychology, offering readers an in-depth understanding of the key theories and empirical findings in the field. We start with the foundational concepts of cognitive psychology, including memory, learning, and perception, before moving into more complex topics such as decision-making, social cognition, and cognitive dysfunction. Throughout the book, case studies and real-life examples illustrate how these cognitive processes unfold in everyday life, while cutting-edge research highlights the innovations and challenges shaping the future of the field.

One of the defining aspects of this book is its emphasis on the intersection between cognition and other fields, such as neuroscience, mental health, and artificial intelligence. By bridging these areas, we aim to present a comprehensive understanding of how cognition influences and is influenced by various domains, offering readers a multidimensional view of human nature. Additionally, we explore the ways in which technology is reshaping the way we think and learn, with discussions on the implications of the digital age on cognition and future directions in cognitive psychology.

This book is intended for students, researchers, and practitioners in psychology, neuroscience, education, and related fields, as well as anyone interested in understanding the complexities of the human mind. Whether you are looking to deepen your understanding of cognitive psychology or simply curious about how cognition shapes our daily lives, *Cognitive Footprints* offers a thoughtful and engaging exploration of one of the most fascinating and rapidly evolving areas of scientific inquiry.

We hope this book will inspire readers to reflect on the cognitive processes that guide their own thinking and behaviour, and to appreciate the profound influence cognition has on shaping the human experience.

Authors:

Prof. Dr. Anu Kant Mital

Overview of the Book

Cognitive Footprints: Tracing Human Nature Through Psychology is a comprehensive exploration of the cognitive processes that underlie human behaviour and thought. This book delves into the intricate workings of the human mind, offering a deep dive into the mechanisms of memory, perception, decision-making, problem-solving, and social cognition, all of which play pivotal roles in shaping how we interpret the world around us and interact with others.

The book is structured into nine detailed chapters, each focusing on a critical aspect of cognitive psychology. From foundational concepts in the early chapters to more complex ideas about emotion, cognition, and mental health, the book presents a clear and accessible journey through the field. It is designed to appeal to students, scholars, and anyone interested in understanding the interplay between cognition and human behaviour.

- Chapter 1: The Foundations of Human Cognition introduces the core concepts of cognitive psychology, including its historical development, key theories, and the integration of neuroscience into understanding mental processes.
- Chapter 2: Memory and Learning: The Cognitive Architecture focuses on how we acquire, retain, and retrieve information. It discusses various theories of memory, including the multi-store model and the working memory model, while also exploring techniques to enhance learning and memory.
- Chapter 3: Perception: The Lens Through Which We See the World delves into how the brain interprets sensory data and creates coherent experiences. It includes insights into how culture, experience, and cognitive illusions influence how we perceive reality.
- Chapter 4: Decision-Making and Problem-Solving explores the cognitive processes involved in making choices and solving problems. It examines the role of heuristics and cognitive biases and

their impact on human decision-making, as well as the cognitive styles that shape problem-solving strategies.

- **Chapter 5: The Role of Emotion in Cognition** investigates the interrelationship between emotions and cognitive processes. The chapter highlights how emotions influence memory, attention, and decision-making, and explores the concept of emotional intelligence and its role in social interactions.
- **Chapter 6: Cognitive Development Across the Lifespan** provides an overview of how cognitive abilities evolve throughout life. It includes major theories of cognitive development, from Piaget's stages of cognitive development to Vygotsky's sociocultural theory, and examines cognitive changes during childhood, adolescence, and old age.
- **Chapter 7: Social Cognition: Understanding Others and Ourselves** examines how we interpret and understand the behaviour of others. This chapter covers social perception, attribution theory, self-identity, and the role of empathy in social interactions.
- **Chapter 8: Cognitive Dysfunction and Mental Health** focuses on how cognitive processes are affected by mental health disorders. It highlights cognitive dysfunctions in conditions such as ADHD, depression, anxiety, and dementia, and explores the effectiveness of cognitive therapies in treatment.
- **Chapter 9: The Future of Cognitive Psychology** looks ahead at the future directions in cognitive psychology, with particular emphasis on the integration of artificial intelligence, advances in neuroscience, and the impact of digital technology on cognitive functions.

Each chapter is designed to provide readers with a deep understanding of the key concepts, theories, and research that have shaped cognitive psychology.

Table of Contents

1

The Foundations of Human Cognition

1.1 Understanding Cognitive Psychology

Cognitive psychology is the study of mental processes such as attention, memory, perception, and problem-solving. It focuses on how individuals acquire, process, and store information, ultimately affecting their behaviours and decisions.

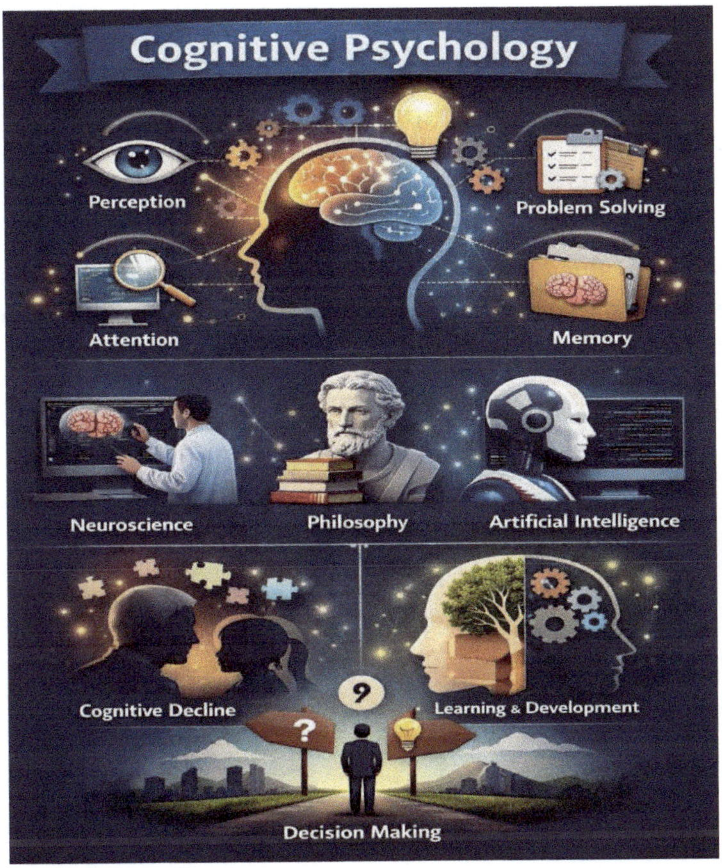

Cognitive psychology is the branch of psychology that focuses on understanding the mental processes that influence human behaviour. These processes include attention, memory, perception, problem-solving, reasoning, and decision-making. Unlike behaviourism, which primarily concentrates on observable actions, cognitive psychology delves into the internal mental mechanisms that guide those actions.

Cognitive psychology emerged in the mid-20th century as a response to behaviourism, which neglected the complexities of the mind in Favor of studying outward behaviours. Researchers in cognitive psychology aim to uncover how individuals acquire, process, and store information, as well as how these processes influence their interactions with the world around them.

The field draws from various disciplines, including neuroscience, which examines the brain's physical structures and functions; philosophy, which explores the nature of knowledge and perception; and computer science, which provides insights into the functioning of artificial intelligence systems that can mimic human cognition. Cognitive psychology uses models and frameworks to study mental processes, such as how individuals interpret sensory input and how they make decisions based on the information they process.

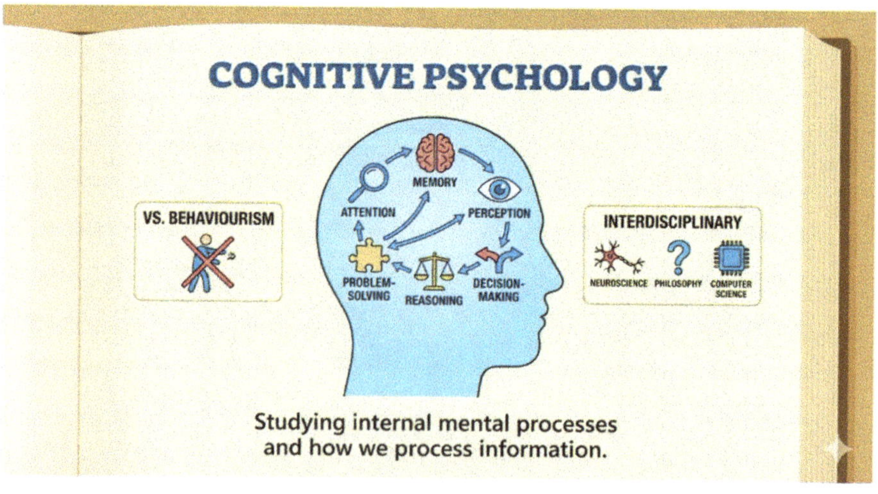

Moreover, cognitive psychology not only examines normal cognitive functions but also explores cognitive decline in conditions like Alzheimer's disease, as well as the developmental changes in cognition throughout a person's life. By understanding how cognitive processes operate and evolve, cognitive psychology offers valuable insights into human learning, memory retention, and the challenges associated with cognitive impairments.

1.2 The Evolution of the Mind

The evolution of the human mind is a critical area in understanding cognitive psychology. Our cognitive abilities have evolved over millions of years to adapt to environmental challenges. Early human cognition was shaped by the necessity of survival, leading to the development of complex skills such as problem-solving, language, and social interaction.

The evolution of the human mind is a fundamental aspect of cognitive psychology, as it helps explain how our cognitive abilities developed over time to meet the challenges posed by the environment. Early human cognition was primarily driven by the need to survive in harsh conditions, leading to the development of essential cognitive skills such as problem-solving, memory, and social interaction. These skills were crucial for early humans to navigate their surroundings, hunt for food, build shelter, and form social bonds.

Over millions of years, the human brain has undergone significant changes in size and structure, allowing for more complex mental processes. The expansion of the neocortex, which is involved in higher-level functions such as reasoning, abstract thinking, and decision-making, is one of the key evolutionary developments that set humans apart from other species. This growth in brain size and complexity allowed humans to develop advanced cognitive functions like language, planning, and emotional regulation, which are essential for modern-day interactions and problem-solving.

From an evolutionary perspective, our cognitive abilities did not emerge in isolation; rather, they evolved in response to the demands of our environment. For example, the development of language allowed for more sophisticated communication, which facilitated social cooperation and the sharing of knowledge. Problem-solving abilities enabled humans to adapt to changing environments and create innovative tools. Additionally, social interaction and empathy evolved to foster group cohesion and support survival within social groups.

Studying the evolution of the human brain provides valuable insights into the foundations of cognitive psychology. By understanding how our brain's architecture evolved, researchers can better comprehend how modern humans process information, make decisions, and interact with the world. This evolutionary perspective sheds light on why certain cognitive functions, such as memory and attention, are so critical to human behaviour and how they have been shaped by millions of years of adaptation.

1.3 Cognitive Functions and Structures

Cognitive functions such as attention, perception, memory, and decision-making are fundamental to human thought. These functions are supported by various brain structures, each responsible for different aspects of cognitive processing.

Cognitive functions such as attention, perception, memory, and decision-making are essential components of human thought and behaviour. These functions allow individuals to process information, make judgments, recall experiences, and respond to their environments in adaptive ways. Behind these complex mental activities, various brain structures work together, each contributing to different aspects of cognitive processing. Understanding how these functions interact and the brain structures that support them provides valuable insights into the workings of the human mind.

Attention and the Brain:

Attention is a critical cognitive function that allows individuals to focus on relevant stimuli while ignoring distractions. The brain's attention system involves several areas, including the parietal lobe and the anterior cingulate cortex. These areas help direct focus, prioritize tasks, and regulate the number of cognitive resources allocated to specific activities. Attention is essential for tasks such as reading, driving, or engaging in conversations, where selective focus is required to navigate complex environments.

Perception and Sensory Processing:

Perception refers to the brain's ability to interpret sensory input from the environment. This function involves the integration of information from the five senses-sight, hearing, touch, taste, and smell-to create meaningful representations of the world. The occipital lobe plays a key role in processing visual information, while the temporal lobe is responsible for processing auditory input. Perception is not a passive process; it requires active interpretation and is influenced by past experiences, expectations, and attentional focus.

Memory Formation and the Hippocampus:

Memory is a foundational cognitive function that enables individuals to store, retrieve, and use information. The hippocampus, located in the temporal lobe, is crucial for memory formation, particularly in the consolidation of short-term memories into long-term memories. It also plays a role in spatial memory, helping individuals navigate through their environment. Memory is divided into different types, such as episodic memory (events and experiences), semantic memory (facts and knowledge), and procedural memory (skills and habits). The intricate workings of the hippocampus and other memory-related regions, such as the amygdala, highlight the brain's capacity to encode and recall vast amounts of information.

Decision-Making and the Prefrontal Cortex:

Decision-making is the cognitive process by which individuals evaluate options and make choices. The prefrontal cortex, located at the front of the brain, is heavily involved in this process. It is responsible for higher-order executive functions, including planning, reasoning, judgment, and impulse control. The prefrontal cortex integrates information from other brain regions to assess potential outcomes and guide behaviour. This area of the brain helps individuals weigh pros and cons, set goals, and make decisions based on future consequences. Damage to the prefrontal cortex can lead to impairments in decision-making, leading to impulsive or poorly thought-out choices.

Coordinated Interaction of Cognitive Functions:
Although each of these cognitive functions is supported by specific brain structures, they do not operate in isolation. Attention, perception, memory, and decision-making work together seamlessly to allow individuals to interact with the world effectively. For instance, when making a decision, an individual must first attend to relevant information, perceive the options available, recall previous experiences (memory), and finally evaluate the best course of action (decision-making). The coordination of these functions enables individuals to process complex information quickly and accurately.

1.4 The Role of Neuroscience in Cognitive Psychology

Neuroscience plays a vital role in cognitive psychology by examining how brain activity correlates with cognitive functions. Techniques such as functional magnetic resonance imaging (fMRI) and
electroencephalography (EEG) allow researchers to observe real-time brain activity during tasks involving memory, problem-solving, or decision-making.

Neuroscience plays a crucial role in cognitive psychology by providing a biological framework for understanding how brain activity is linked to cognitive functions. Cognitive psychology focuses on mental processes like attention, memory, perception, and decision-making, and neuroscience helps to elucidate the neural mechanisms that underlie these processes. By examining the brain's structure and activity, neuroscience contributes significantly to the understanding of cognition, allowing researchers to bridge the gap between abstract mental processes and the tangible biological functions of the brain.

Techniques for Studying Brain Activity:
Advances in neuroimaging techniques have greatly enhanced the ability to observe brain activity in real time. One of the most widely used methods is functional magnetic resonance imaging (fMRI), which measures changes in blood flow in the brain, providing a detailed map of brain activity during

cognitive tasks. fMRI allows researchers to identify which areas of the brain are activated when individuals perform tasks related to memory, problem-solving, or decision-making. By observing these patterns of brain activation, scientists can gain insights into how different regions of the brain collaborate to process information.

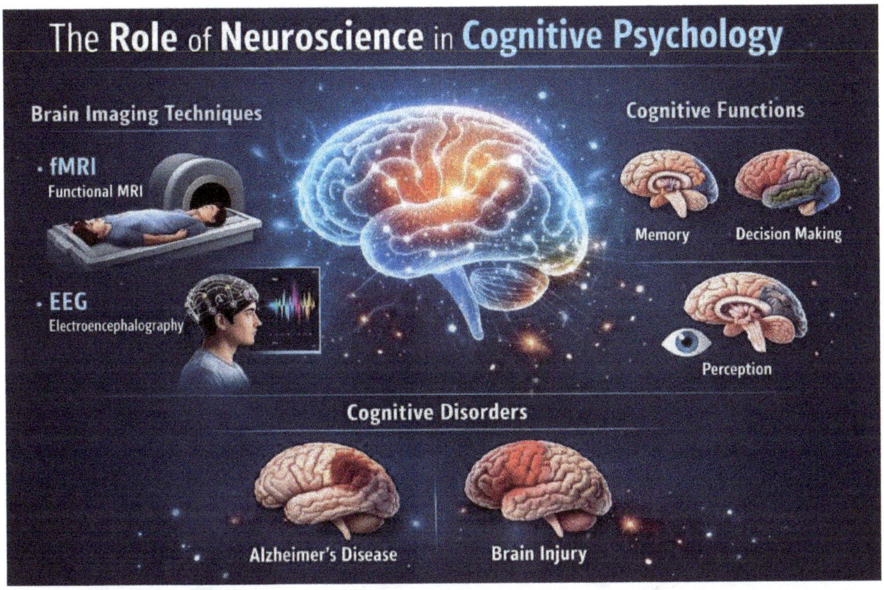

Another valuable technique is electroencephalography (EEG), which measures electrical activity in the brain through electrodes placed on the scalp. Unlike fMRI, which provides detailed images of brain structures, EEG offers a time-sensitive view of brain activity, making it useful for studying the temporal dynamics of cognitive processes. EEG is particularly effective for understanding the timing of neural responses, such as how quickly the brain reacts to stimuli during tasks involving attention or perception.

Understanding the Neural Basis of Cognition:

Neuroscience helps cognitive psychologists understand the biological basis of cognitive functions. For example, research has shown that the hippocampus is crucial for memory formation, the prefrontal cortex plays a key role in decision-making and executive functions, and the occipital lobe is responsible for processing visual information. By identifying these brain regions and studying their activity, researchers can build an integrated model of how thought and behaviour arise from brain activity.

Cognitive Disorders and Brain Damage:

Neuroscience also plays a critical role in understanding cognitive disorders. Damage to specific brain regions can lead to impairments in cognitive functions. For example, individuals with damage to the hippocampus may experience severe memory loss, while damage to the prefrontal cortex can result in difficulties with decision-making, impulse control, and problem-solving. Neuroscientific research provides insights into how such brain injuries or diseases, such as Alzheimer's disease or traumatic brain injury, affect cognitive abilities.

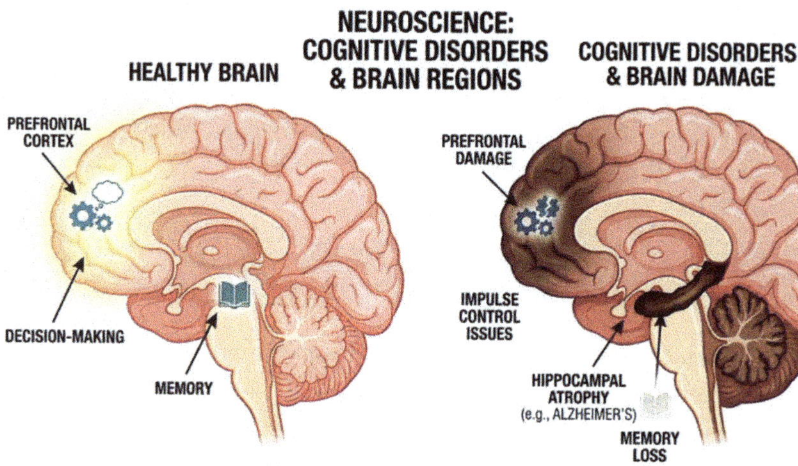

Through brain imaging studies, neuroscientists can track changes in brain activity and structure in individuals with cognitive impairments, leading to better diagnosis, treatment, and rehabilitation strategies. For example, research on patients with Alzheimer's disease has shown that the hippocampus undergoes significant atrophy, which correlates with memory deficits. This understanding has guided the development of therapeutic interventions aimed at slowing the progression of the disease.

Multiple Choice Questions (MCQs)

1. Which of the following cognitive functions is primarily responsible for focusing attention on specific tasks or stimuli?

A) Perception
B) Memory
C) Attention
D) Problem-solving

Answer: C) Attention

2. The hippocampus is primarily involved in which of the following cognitive processes?

A) Problem-solving
B) Language comprehension
C) Memory formation
D) Decision-making

Answer: C) Memory formation

3. Which brain region is most associated with higher-level functions such as planning, decision-making, and impulse control?

A) Occipital lobe
B) Prefrontal cortex
C) Temporal lobe
D) Hippocampus

Answer: B) Prefrontal cortex

4. What does functional magnetic resonance imaging (fMRI) measure in the brain?

A) Electrical activity in neurons
B) Blood flow changes related to brain activity
C) Size of different brain regions
D) Brain cell connections

Answer: B) Blood flow changes related to brain activity

5. Which of the following cognitive disorders is associated with damage to the hippocampus?

A) Alzheimer's disease
B) Parkinson's disease
C) Schizophrenia
D) Huntington's disease

Answer: A) Alzheimer's disease

Short Answer Questions

1. What is cognitive psychology, and how does it differ from behaviourism?
2. Which brain structure is most associated with memory formation, and what role does it play in cognition?
3. What is the primary function of the prefrontal cortex in cognitive processing?
4. How do techniques like fMRI and EEG help researchers study brain activity during cognitive tasks?
5. What role does attention play in cognitive functions, and why is it essential for effective problem-solving?
6. What is the significance of understanding the evolution of the human mind in the context of cognitive psychology?

Long Answer Questions

1. Discuss the relationship between cognitive functions such as attention, memory, and decision-making, and explain how different brain structures support these functions.
2. Explain the role of neuroscience in cognitive psychology, including how brain imaging techniques like fMRI and EEG contribute to

understanding mental processes. Provide examples of how brain damage can affect cognitive abilities.

3. Describe the evolution of the human mind and how early human cognitive abilities, such as problem-solving and social interaction, were shaped by survival needs. How has brain size and complexity evolved to accommodate more advanced cognitive functions?

4. What is the connection between memory formation and the hippocampus? Discuss how research in cognitive psychology and neuroscience has provided insights into the different types of memory and their neural underpinnings.

5. Evaluate the significance of cognitive functions in daily life. How do attention, perception, and memory work together to help individuals navigate and interpret their environment effectively? Use real-life examples to illustrate the interplay between these functions.

6. Discuss how cognitive disorders, such as Alzheimer's disease, highlight the importance of specific brain regions in maintaining cognitive functions. How can the study of these disorders enhance our understanding of normal cognitive processes?

2

Memory and Learning: The Cognitive Architecture

2.1 Theories of Memory

Memory is a cornerstone of human cognition. Several theories attempt to explain how memory works, such as the multi-store model, which divides memory into sensory, short-term, and long-term stores. The working memory model further refines this by proposing that short-term memory is an active system with components for processing auditory and visual-spatial information.

Memory is an essential aspect of human cognition, serving as the foundation for learning, decision-making, and problem-solving. Multiple theories have been proposed to explain how memory functions, each contributing to a deeper understanding of its processes.

One influential theory is the **multi-store model of memory** , which was first introduced by Atkinson and Shiffrin in 1968. This model divides memory into three distinct stores: sensory memory, short-term memory, and long-term memory. Sensory memory captures fleeting impressions of the environment and holds them for a very brief period (milliseconds to seconds). Information that is paid attention to moves from sensory memory to short-term memory, which has limited capacity and retains information for a few seconds to minutes. If this information is rehearsed, it can be transferred into long-term memory, where it is stored more permanently.

An extension of the multi-store model is the **working memory model** , proposed by Baddeley and Hitch in 1974. This model refines the concept of short-term memory by suggesting that it is an active system with separate components for processing different types of information. These include the phonological loop, which processes auditory information; the visuospatial sketchpad, which handles visual and spatial data; and the central executive, which coordinates and integrates these components. Working memory emphasizes that memory is not just a passive repository but an active, dynamic system where information is actively manipulated.

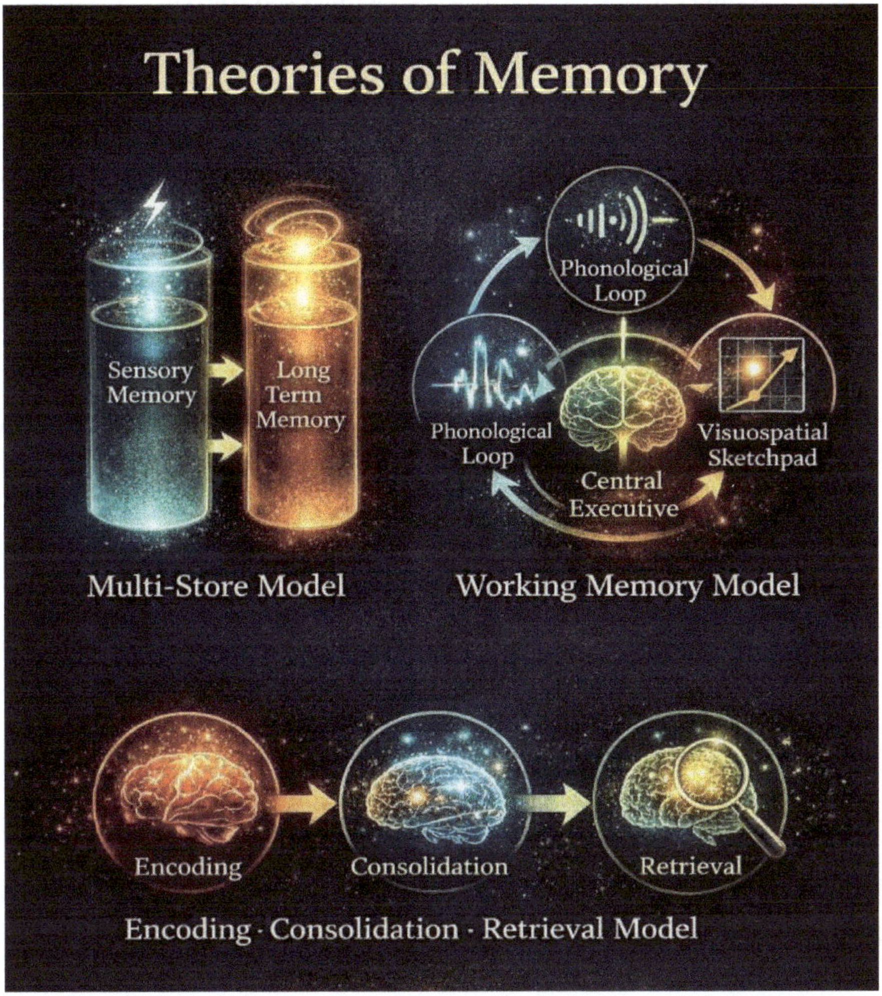

More recent theories of memory, such as the **encoding, consolidation, and retrieval model** , focus on the stages of memory processing. **Encoding** refers to the process of transforming sensory input into a form that can be stored. **Consolidation** involves the stabilization of memories over time, particularly through rehearsal and the formation of neural connections. **Retrieval** is the process of accessing stored information when needed. This model suggests that memory is not a perfect recording of past events but rather a reconstructive process, influenced by various factors like attention, prior knowledge, and the context in which the memory is retrieved.

These theories illustrate the complexity of memory and highlight the fact that memory is not a static storage system but an active and dynamic cognitive process. By integrating these theories, psychologists continue to gain insights into how memories are formed, retained, and retrieved, as well as the factors that influence memory accuracy and recall.

2.2 The Process of Learning

Learning involves the acquisition of new information, skills, or behaviours. Cognitive learning theories suggest that learning occurs when individuals actively construct their understanding of the world through experiences. Classical conditioning (Pavlov) and operant conditioning (Skinner) are foundational learning theories.

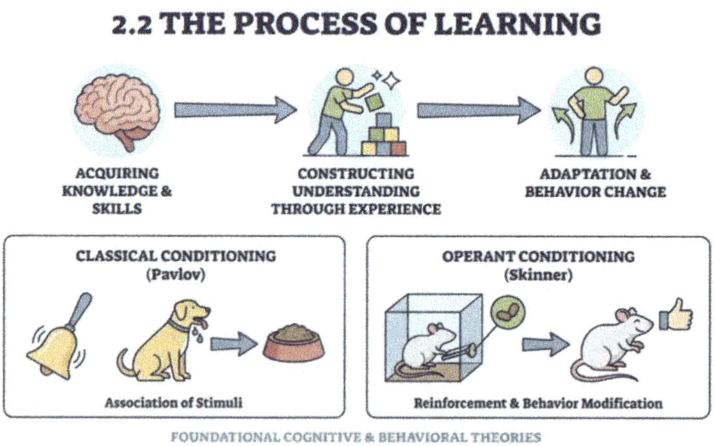

Learning is a fundamental process through which individuals acquire new information, skills, or behaviours. It involves the active construction of knowledge and the ability to adapt and modify one's understanding of the world based on experiences. Several cognitive learning theories attempt to explain how this process works, with each theory contributing insights into different aspects of learning.

One of the most well-known learning theories is **classical conditioning**, introduced by Ivan Pavlov. This theory focuses on the association between a neutral stimulus and an unconditioned stimulus to produce a conditioned response. Pavlov's famous experiment with dogs demonstrated how a neutral stimulus (such as a bell) could eventually trigger a salivation response when paired with food. This form of learning is passive and based on associations, where behaviours are elicited by environmental stimuli.

Another foundational learning theory is **operant conditioning**, developed by B.F. Skinner. In contrast to classical conditioning, operant conditioning emphasizes the role of reinforcement and punishment in shaping behaviour. Through positive reinforcement (rewarding desired behaviour) or negative reinforcement (removing an unpleasant stimulus), individuals are more likely to repeat behaviours. On the other hand, behaviours that are punished are less likely to be repeated. Skinner's experiments with animals, such as rats pressing levers for food, demonstrated how behaviour could be shaped through consequences.

In addition to these behavioural theories, **constructivist theories** of learning, particularly those proposed by Jean Piaget and Lev Vygotsky, emphasize the active role of learners in constructing their own knowledge. Piaget's theory of cognitive development suggests that individuals move through distinct stages (sensorimotor, preoperational, concrete operational, and formal operational) as they build on previous knowledge and experiences. According to Piaget, learning occurs as children interact with their environment, actively seeking to make sense of the world around them.

Vygotsky's theory, often referred to as **sociocultural theory**, emphasizes the social nature of learning. Vygotsky argued that learning is deeply influenced by social interactions and cultural tools. The concept of the **zone of proximal development (ZPD)** highlights the difference between what a learner can do independently and what they can achieve with the help of a more knowledgeable person. This interaction helps to bridge the gap between existing knowledge and new learning.

All of these theories highlight the **cognitive aspects** of learning, which involve the encoding, storing, and processing of new information. Learning is not simply about absorbing facts; it is an active, dynamic process where individuals make sense of new information and apply it to solve problems or make decisions. By understanding these processes, we gain insights into how people learn, how knowledge is built, and how new behaviours are acquired and maintained.

2.3 Cognitive Distortions in Memory

While memory is a powerful tool, it is not infallible. Cognitive distortions occur when the mind alters memories based on biases or emotional states. False memories, confabulation, and the Mandela effect are examples of how our recollections can be inaccurate or distorted.

Memory, while a powerful tool for understanding and navigating the world, is not infallible. Cognitive distortions refer to the ways in which our recollections can be altered or influenced by biases, emotions, and external factors. These distortions can lead to inaccuracies in memory, causing us to remember events differently from how they actually occurred. Cognitive psychology delves into the mechanisms behind these distortions, exploring how various factors can reshape our memories over time.

One of the most well-known forms of memory distortion is the phenomenon of **false memories**, where individuals recall events that never actually happened or recall them in a way that differs significantly from the truth. False memories can be triggered by suggestion, misleading information, or personal biases, and they highlight how susceptible our memories are to outside influences. This can happen consciously, through suggestions or leading questions, or unconsciously, as memories are reconstructed and filled in by the brain.

Confabulation is another form of memory distortion, where individuals unintentionally fabricate details to fill gaps in their memory. Unlike lying, confabulation occurs without the intention to deceive. This often happens when people experience memory lapses or confusion and attempt to "make up" missing information to make sense of their recollections. Confabulated memories may seem convincing, but they can be entirely fabricated, with no basis in reality.

The **Mandela effect** is a curious example of collective memory distortion, where large groups of people recall an event or detail incorrectly. Named after Nelson Mandela, whose death was falsely remembered by some as occurring in the 1980s, the Mandela effect highlights how collective recollections can be shaped by shared misinformation or cultural influences. This phenomenon often leads to widespread misremembering of facts, like the incorrect recall of product logos or historical events.

2.4 Enhancing Memory and Learning Techniques

There are various strategies to enhance memory and improve learning efficiency. Mnemonic devices, such as acronyms or visualization techniques, help encode information more effectively. Spaced repetition, where information is reviewed at increasing intervals, is another method that has proven effective in promoting long-term retention. Cognitive

psychologists also study the role of sleep in memory consolidation, highlighting how adequate rest strengthens newly acquired memories.

Memory and learning are complex processes, but there are several strategies that can enhance these cognitive functions and improve learning efficiency. These techniques leverage cognitive principles to optimize the way we acquire, store, and retain knowledge. By using various methods to improve encoding, retention, and retrieval, individuals can boost their ability to learn new information and recall it when needed.

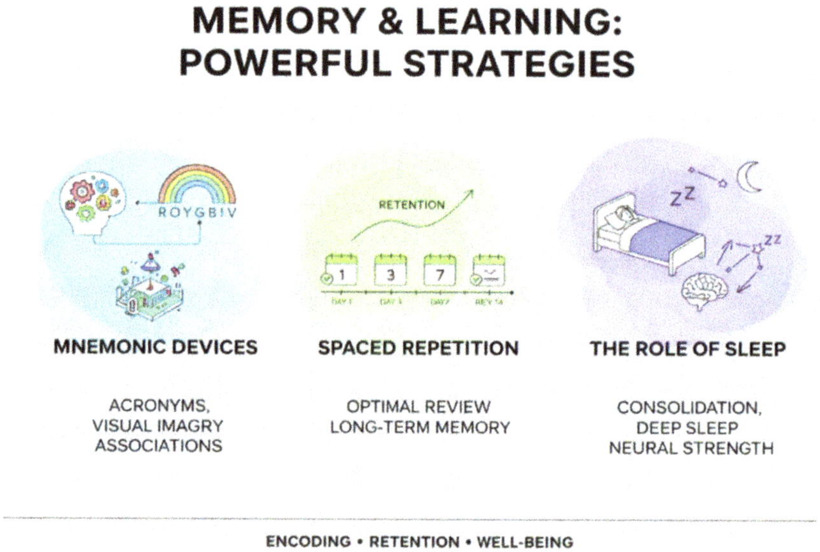

One effective strategy is the use of **mnemonic devices**. These are techniques that aid in the encoding and retrieval of information by creating associations. Mnemonics can take several forms, such as acronyms, rhymes, or visual imagery. For instance, the acronym "ROYGBIV" is commonly used to remember the colours of the rainbow (Red, Orange, Yellow, Green, Blue, Indigo, Violet). Visualization techniques are another form of mnemonic, where individuals create vivid mental images to represent concepts, making them easier to remember. For example, to remember a list of items, a person might visualize each item in a particular place or scenario. Mnemonics make abstract information more tangible and easier to retrieve by creating stronger connections in the brain.

Another powerful technique for enhancing memory is **spaced repetition** . This method involves reviewing information at increasing intervals, which has been shown to significantly improve long-term retention. Instead of cramming information all at once, spaced repetition encourages repeated exposure to material over time. The spacing effect, first demonstrated by Hermann Ebbinghaus in the 19th century, suggests that learning is more effective when information is reviewed at spaced intervals rather than in a single, continuous study session. For example, a student might review material the day after learning it, then again a few days later, and then a week later. This method strengthens memory consolidation and reduces forgetting, making it ideal for studying and language learning.

The role of **sleep** in memory consolidation is another critical aspect of enhancing learning. Research in cognitive psychology has shown that sleep plays a vital role in transferring newly learned information from short-term memory to long-term memory. During sleep, particularly during deep sleep and REM (Rapid Eye Movement) stages, the brain processes and consolidates information learned throughout the day. Adequate rest helps strengthen neural connections, making it easier to recall and apply new knowledge. Studies have shown that individuals who get a full night's sleep after learning a new task perform better on memory tests than those who stay awake. Therefore, ensuring proper sleep is a crucial element in optimizing memory retention.

Elaboration and Self-Testing are additional techniques that can enhance learning. Elaboration involves making connections between new information and existing knowledge, which strengthens understanding and memory. For instance, when learning a new concept, a student might relate it to real-world examples or previous experiences. This deepens comprehension and creates multiple retrieval pathways for the information. Self-testing, or practicing retrieval, is another valuable technique. By regularly testing oneself on the material being studied, learners reinforce their memory and improve their ability to recall the information when needed.

Active Learning is a dynamic approach to improving memory and understanding. Rather than passively reading or listening, active learning involves engaging with the material through activities such as discussion, teaching others, or applying concepts to real-world problems. Active learning requires higher levels of cognitive processing, which strengthens memory and enhances learning.

Multiple Choice Questions (MCQs)

1. Which of the following models divides memory into sensory memory, short-term memory, and long-term memory?

a) Working Memory Model
b) Multi-Store Model
c) Constructivist Model
d) Encoding, Consolidation, and Retrieval Model

Answer:
b) Multi-Store Model

2. In the Working Memory Model, which component is responsible for processing auditory information?

a) Visuospatial Sketchpad
b) Central Executive
c) Phonological Loop
d) Episodic Buffer

Answer:
c) Phonological Loop

3. Which of the following techniques involves reviewing information at increasing intervals to improve long-term retention?

a) Mnemonic Devices
b) Spaced Repetition

c) Elaborative Rehearsal
d) Chunking

Answer:
b) Spaced Repetition

4. According to cognitive psychology, how does sleep contribute to memory?

a) It helps encode information into short-term memory.
b) It prevents new memories from being consolidated.
c) It plays a key role in transferring new information from short-term memory to long-term memory.
d) It enhances memory retrieval but not consolidation.

Answer:
c) It plays a key role in transferring new information from short-term memory to long-term memory.

5. Which of the following is NOT considered a form of cognitive distortion in memory?

a) False Memories
b) Confabulation
c) Spaced Repetition
d) The Mandela Effect

Answer:
c) Spaced Repetition

Short Answer Questions

1. What is the difference between the Multi-Store Model and the Working Memory Model of memory?
2. How does spaced repetition improve long-term memory retention?
3. What role does sleep play in memory consolidation?

4. What is a mnemonic device, and how does it help in memory?
5. What is the Mandela Effect in relation to cognitive distortions in memory?
6. Why is confirmation bias considered a memory distortion?

Long Answer Questions

1. Explain the concept of false memories and how they can be created through suggestion and leading questions. Provide examples of how false memories might manifest in everyday life.
2. Discuss the role of cognitive psychology in understanding how memory and learning work. How do cognitive theories explain the process of encoding, storing, and retrieving information?
3. Describe the process of elaboration in learning and its role in improving memory retention. How does connecting new information to prior knowledge enhance cognitive learning?
4. How does cognitive distortion, like the Mandela Effect, impact collective memory, and what are the implications of these distortions in legal or clinical settings?
5. Explain the importance of active learning in memory enhancement and its impact on retention. Provide examples of how active learning techniques can be implemented in educational settings.
6. Discuss the concept of cognitive load and how it affects memory retention during the learning process. What strategies can be used to manage cognitive load and enhance learning efficiency?

3

Perception: The Lens Through Which We See the World

3.1 The Sensory Systems and Perception

Perception begins with the sensory systems-sight, hearing, taste, smell, and touch-which gather raw data from the environment. This sensory information is then processed by the brain, leading to perceptual experiences.

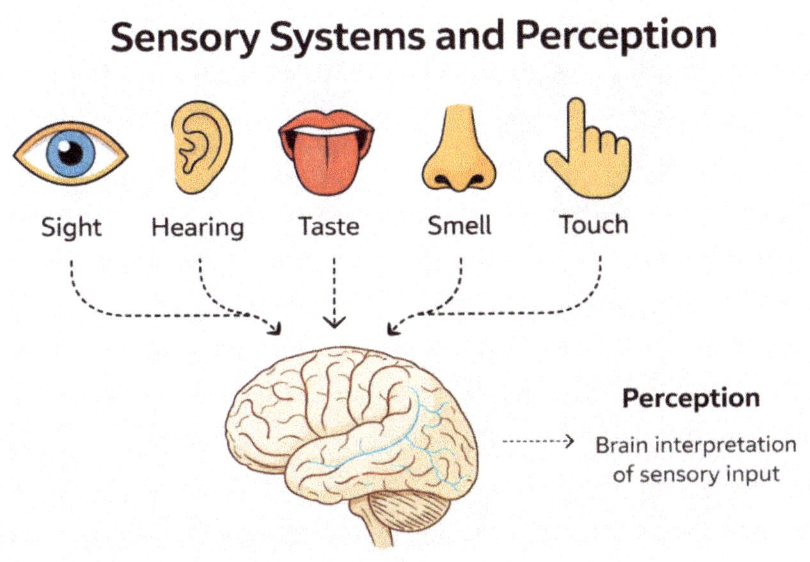

Perception starts with the sensory systems-sight, hearing, taste, smell, and touch-which collect raw information from the external world. These senses act as receptors, picking up stimuli like light, sound waves, chemicals, and pressure, converting them into signals that the brain can process. Once the sensory data is gathered, the brain interprets it to form perceptions, which are our conscious experiences of the world.

However, perception is not just a simple reflection of external stimuli. The brain's interpretation of sensory input is shaped by various factors such as prior knowledge, experiences, expectations, and attention. For example, two individuals might perceive the same event differently based on their past experiences or cultural backgrounds, highlighting how subjective perception can be.

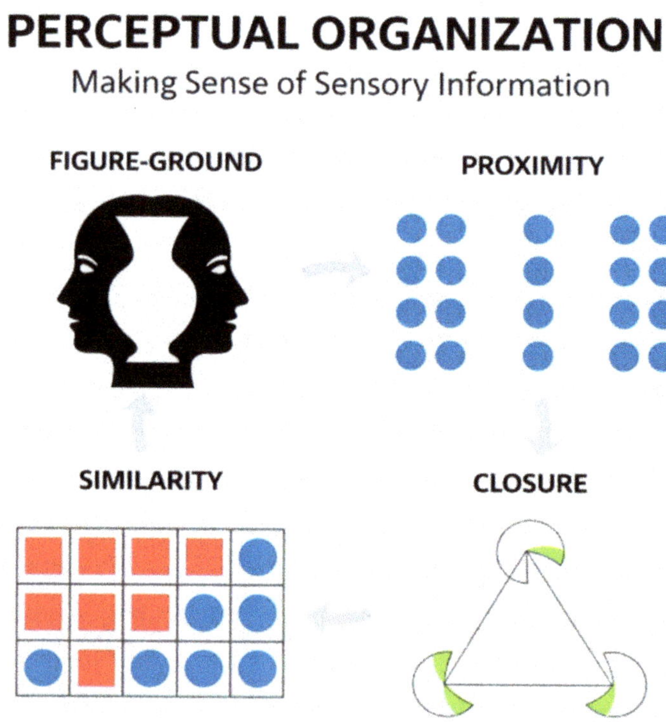

Cognitive psychology examines how these sensory systems work together to create a unified perception of the environment. It also studies how the brain processes sensory data to build our mental representation of reality. Additionally, deficiencies or dysfunctions in the sensory systems can lead to perceptual disorders, where individuals may perceive the world inaccurately.

Examples of such disorders include visual or auditory impairments, where the brain struggles to correctly interpret the sensory information it receives.

3.2 Perceptual Organization

Perceptual organization refers to the brain's ability to make sense of sensory information by organizing it into meaningful patterns or wholes. This process includes principles such as figure-ground segregation (distinguishing objects from their background), proximity, similarity, and closure.

Perceptual organization is the cognitive process by which the brain organizes sensory input into meaningful patterns or wholes. This ability allows us to make sense of the vast amount of sensory information we receive, enabling us to recognize and interpret objects, shapes, and events in our environment. The brain does not process each sensory detail in isolation; instead, it groups the elements together to form coherent perceptions.

Key principles of perceptual organization include **figure-ground segregation**, which helps us distinguish objects (figures) from their background (ground). This principle is essential for recognizing and isolating objects within a complex visual scene. For example, in a crowded room, we focus on one person while ignoring the background details, like the walls or furniture.

Other important principles include **proximity**, where objects that are close together are perceived as a group, and **similarity**, where similar objects are grouped together based on shared characteristics such as colour, shape, or size. For instance, in a crowd, we may group people dressed in similar clothing together.

Closure is another principle that suggests the brain tends to complete incomplete shapes or figures, filling in gaps to perceive a whole. For example, if we see a circle with a small gap, our brain will fill in the missing part, perceiving it as a complete circle.

The **Gestalt laws of perceptual organization** highlight how the brain uses these principles to organize sensory stimuli in ways that make the most sense given the context. These laws emphasize the tendency of the mind to simplify complex visual input by grouping related elements together and creating structured patterns.

This ability to organize sensory data is crucial for efficiently navigating the world and understanding complex scenes. It allows us to recognize objects quickly, interpret visual and auditory cues, and respond to our environment in meaningful ways. Without perceptual organization, our perception of the world would be fragmented and overwhelming.

3.3 Cognitive Illusions and Misperceptions

Cognitive illusions are errors in perception that occur when the brain misinterprets sensory data. Optical illusions are a classic example of how perception can deceive us, demonstrating the brain's active role in constructing reality. Cognitive illusions can also be more complex, involving misinterpretations of size, colour, or depth.

Cognitive illusions are errors in perception that occur when the brain misinterprets sensory information, leading to a distorted or incorrect understanding of the environment. A well-known example of this phenomenon is optical illusions, which vividly demonstrate how the brain actively constructs reality rather than passively receiving sensory data. In these cases, the sensory information is processed in ways that lead to an inaccurate or misleading perception, even though the stimuli are clear and consistent.

Cognitive illusions can go beyond simple visual distortions. They may involve misperceptions of size, colour, depth, or even spatial relationships. For example, the well-known *Ames room* illusion creates the impression that people or objects appear to shrink or grow depending on their position within the room, even though they are actually the same size. This happens because the brain uses contextual cues, like depth and perspective, which can be manipulated to create a false perception of reality.

These misperceptions highlight how the brain relies on **heuristics**-mental shortcuts or rules of thumb- to process vast amounts of sensory information quickly. Heuristics are generally useful in making quick decisions or judgments, but they can sometimes lead to errors. For instance, the size-**weight illusion**, where a lighter object appears heavier than a larger one, occurs because the brain uses relative size and expectations to judge weight, leading to an inaccurate perception.

Understanding cognitive illusions and misperceptions is important for cognitive psychologists, as they offer insights into the limitations and biases in human perception. These illusions reveal that perception is not a flawless mirror of reality but rather a complex, interpretive process influenced by mental shortcuts and prior knowledge. Studying these errors helps researchers better understand the mechanisms of perception and how the brain processes information, ultimately shedding light on the cognitive biases that shape our everyday experiences.

3.4 The Role of Culture and Experience in Perception

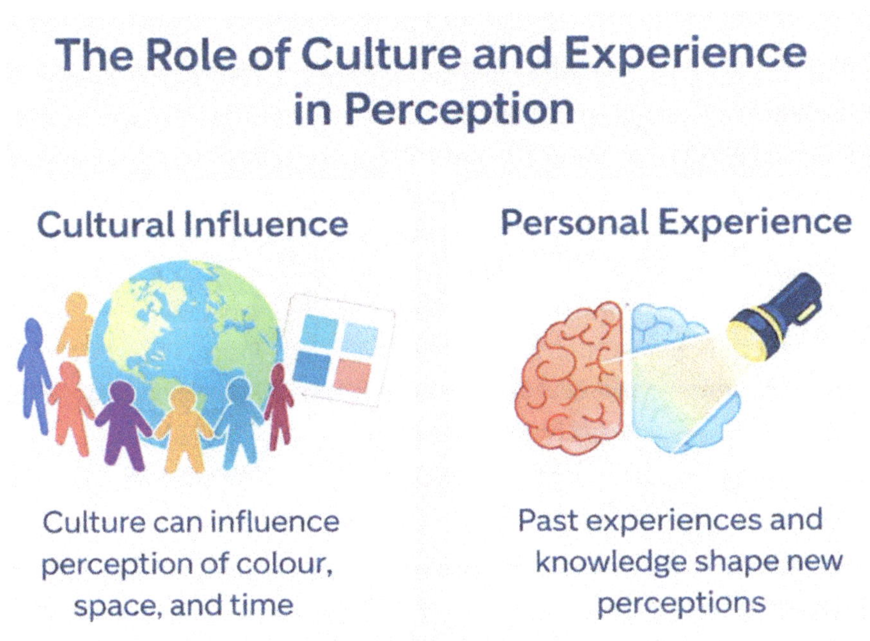

Perception is not only shaped by sensory input but also by cultural background and personal experiences. Cultural differences can influence how individuals perceive colour, space, and time.

Concept	Description	Key Principles/Examples
Sensory Systems and Perception	Perception begins with the sensory systems (sight, hearing, taste, smell, touch) gathering raw data, which is processed by the brain to create perceptual experiences.	**Brain's interpretation influenced by:** Prior experiences, expectations, attention, etc.
Perceptual Organization	The brain organizes sensory information into meaningful patterns or wholes, using principles like figure-ground segregation, proximity, similarity, and closure.	**Gestalt Laws of Perceptual Organization** - Grouping stimuli based on context.
Cognitive Illusions and Misperceptions	Cognitive illusions are errors in perception caused by misinterpretation of sensory data. Optical illusions demonstrate how perception can deceive us.	**Heuristics** - Mental shortcuts used by the brain that can lead to misinterpretations.
Role of Culture and Experience in Perception	Perception is influenced by cultural background and personal experiences, which shape how we interpret sensory information.	**Top-down Processing** - Prior knowledge and expectations influence perception.

Perception is a complex process that involves more than just the sensory input we receive from the environment; it is also heavily influenced by cultural background and personal experiences. These factors shape how we interpret and make sense of the world around us, highlighting that perception is not a passive experience but an active, interpretive one.

Cultural Influence on Perception:

Cultural differences can significantly affect how we perceive various aspects of our environment, such as colour, space, and time. For instance, research has shown that people from different linguistic backgrounds may perceive colours in unique ways. In some languages, certain colours are grouped together under one term, which can affect how individuals distinguish between those colours. For example, speakers of languages with more specific colour terms, such as Russian, may be better at distinguishing shades of blue, as their language provides distinct words for light blue and dark blue whereas English speakers use one word ("blue") for both.

Similarly, cultural norms can shape how individuals perceive space and time. In some cultures, time is viewed as linear, with a clear progression from past to future, while other cultures may have a more cyclical view of time. This cultural framework influences how people organize their activities, manage deadlines, or even interpret past events.

The Role of Personal Experience:

In addition to culture, personal experiences also play a crucial role in shaping perception. These experiences, such as prior knowledge or expectations, influence how we interpret incoming sensory information. This concept is referred to as top-down processing, where the brain uses previously acquired knowledge to guide the perception of new stimuli. For example, when we look at a partially obscured object, our brain fills in the missing details based on past experiences, allowing us to recognize the object despite the lack of complete information.

Multiple Choice Questions (MCQs)

1. Which of the following sensory systems is NOT involved in the process of perception?

a) Sight
b) Hearing
c) Taste
d) Memory

Answer: d) Memory

2. What principle of perceptual organization helps us distinguish objects from their background?

a) Similarity
b) Proximity
c) Closure
d) Figure-ground segregation

Answer: d) Figure-ground segregation

3. Cognitive illusions arise when the brain:

a) Correctly interprets sensory data
b) Misinterprets sensory data
c) Processes information with no prior experiences
d) Ignores sensory information

Answer: b) Misinterprets sensory data

4. The phenomenon where the brain organizes sensory information into meaningful patterns is known as:

a) Sensory adaptation
b) Perceptual organization
c) Sensory gating
d) Cognitive dissonance

Answer: b) Perceptual organization

5. What does "top-down processing" refer to in perception?

a) The process where sensory input is analysed without prior knowledge

b) The brain's use of prior knowledge and expectations to interpret sensory data
c) The perception of depth based on sensory data
d) The sensory processing of the raw data from the environment

Answer: b) The brain's use of prior knowledge and expectations to interpret sensory data

Short Answer Questions

1. What is the role of sensory systems in perception?
2. How does figure-ground segregation contribute to perceptual organization?
3. What is the difference between top-down and bottom-up processing in perception?
4. Explain the concept of cognitive illusions with an example.
5. How does culture influence the way people perceive colour and space?
6. What is the Gestalt principle of closure, and how does it affect perception?

Long Answer Questions

1. Discuss the process of perception, focusing on how the brain integrates sensory data from sight, hearing, taste, smell, and touch to form perceptual experiences.
2. Explain the role of prior experiences and expectations in shaping perception. How does top-down processing influence the way we interpret sensory information in everyday life?
3. Describe the key principles of perceptual organization, such as proximity, similarity, and closure. How do these principles help us make sense of complex visual scenes? Provide real-life examples.

4. Examine the concept of cognitive illusions and how they reveal the limitations of human perception.

5. Explore how cultural differences affect perceptual experiences. How might people from different cultural backgrounds perceive time, space, or colour differently?

6. Analyse the interaction between sensory input and cognitive processes in the development of perceptual disorders. Discuss how deficiencies in sensory systems can lead to misperceptions or illusions, and provide examples of perceptual disorders.

4

Decision-Making and Problem-Solving

4.1 Theories of Decision-Making

Decision-making theories explore how individuals make choices among alternatives. The rational choice theory posits that individuals make

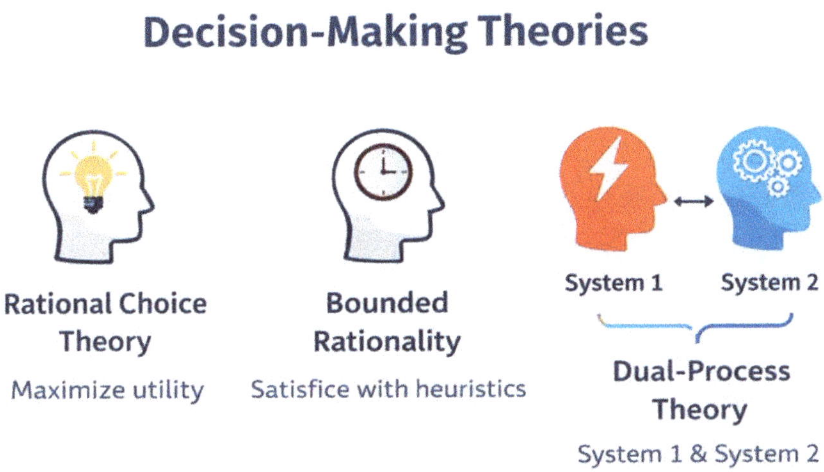

Decision-making theories seek to understand the processes that guide individuals in choosing between different alternatives. These theories explore the cognitive, emotional, and social factors influencing how decisions are made.

1. **Rational Choice Theory** : This theory assumes that individuals make decisions by carefully considering the available options, weighing their costs and benefits, and selecting the one that maximizes utility. It suggests that decision-makers act in a way that is logically sound and based on all available information. While rational choice theory is often applied in economics, it can be criticized for assuming that individuals always have complete

information and make decisions based purely on logic, disregarding the complexities of real-world decision-making.

2. **Bounded Rationality** : Introduced by Herbert Simon, bounded rationality challenges the idea that people always make optimal decisions. It posits that due to cognitive limitations and the constraints of time, individuals often settle for decisions that are "good enough" rather than ideal. In practice, decision-makers may not have access to all relevant information or the ability to process it, so they use heuristics or simplified decision rules to arrive at satisfactory outcomes, rather than optimal ones. This theory recognizes the human tendency to make decisions with incomplete information and within specific constraints.

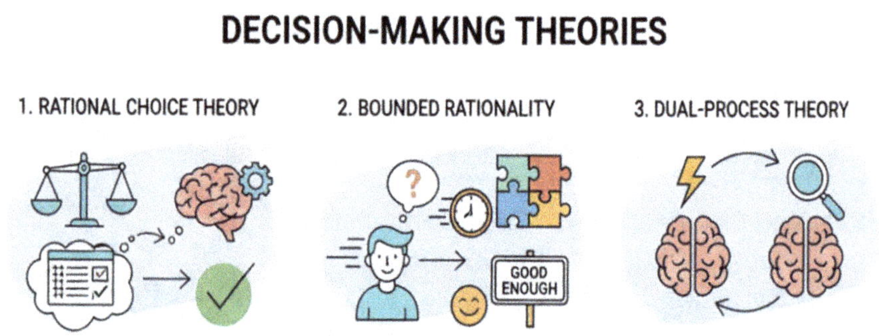

3. **Dual-Process Theory** : Daniel Kahneman's dual-process theory distinguishes between two modes of thinking: System 1 and System 2. System 1 is fast, automatic, and intuitive. It operates unconsciously and quickly, making decisions based on gut feelings, heuristics, and past experiences. On the other hand, System 2 is slower, more deliberate, and analytical. It requires conscious thought and effort, involving logical reasoning and careful evaluation of alternatives. The theory suggests that while System 1 is useful for making quick decisions in familiar situations, System 2 is necessary for more complex, novel, or high-stakes decisions.

These decision-making theories illustrate the variety of cognitive strategies people employ, highlighting how decisions can be influenced by both rational analysis and cognitive limitations, as well as the interplay between emotion, intuition, and reasoning.

4.2 Heuristics and Cognitive Biases

Heuristics are mental shortcuts or rules of thumb that simplify decision-making but can lead to cognitive biases-systematic patterns of deviation from rationality. Common biases include confirmation bias (favouring information that supports pre-existing beliefs) and anchoring bias (relying too heavily on the first piece of information encountered).

Heuristics are mental shortcuts that help individuals make decisions quickly and efficiently by simplifying complex information. These shortcuts are often helpful, especially in situations that demand fast decision-making. However, they can also lead to cognitive biases, which are systematic patterns of deviation from rational judgment. These biases can distort decision-making and lead to flawed outcomes, especially when decisions have significant consequences.

Heuristics

Heuristics are rules of thumb that the brain uses to streamline decision-making processes. They help people make judgments and solve problems quickly, often in situations where time, information, or cognitive resources are limited. However, while heuristics can be efficient, they don't always guarantee the best decision.

For example:

- **Availability Heuristic** : This heuristic is based on the idea that people are more likely to make decisions based on information that is readily available in their memory. If a person has recently heard about a plane crash, they may overestimate the likelihood of an accident occurring on their next flight, despite air travel being statistically safe.
- **Representativeness Heuristic** : This rule of thumb leads people to judge the probability of an event based on how similar it is to a prototype or stereotype. For instance, if someone is shy and introverted, they may be

assumed to be a librarian based on stereotypes, even though there are many other professions they might fit.

Cognitive Biases

Cognitive biases are systematic errors in judgment and decision-making, often resulting from the use of heuristics. These biases can cause individuals to make irrational decisions, and they are particularly problematic in high-stakes environments like healthcare, finance, or legal settings. Some of the most common cognitive biases include:

1. Confirmation Bias :
Confirmation bias occurs when individuals Favor information that confirms their pre-existing beliefs and ignores information that contradicts them. This bias can be particularly problematic because it reinforces existing assumptions, preventing people from considering alternative perspectives or revising their views.

Example: A person who believes that a particular diet is effective may only seek out success stories or positive testimonials, dismissing any evidence that suggests the diet does not work for everyone.

2. Anchoring Bias :
Anchoring bias happens when individuals rely too heavily on the first piece of information they encounter (the "anchor") when making decisions. This initial piece of information serves as a reference point, which can unduly influence subsequent judgments.

Example: If a person is shown a luxury car priced at $50,000, they might perceive a $35,000 car as reasonably priced, even if it is still above their budget. The initial high price set the anchor, affecting their perception of what constitutes a good deal.

3. Overconfidence Bias :
This bias involves individuals overestimating their own knowledge, skills, or abilities. Overconfidence bias can lead to poor decisions because people fail

to adequately consider risks or challenges, believing they know more than they actually do.

Example: A stock investor might overestimate their ability to predict market trends, leading them to make risky investments without fully analysing potential risks.

4. Framing Effect :

The framing effect refers to the way information is presented influencing decision-making. People can react differently depending on whether a situation is framed in terms of potential gains or losses, even if the actual outcomes are the same.

Example: If a medical treatment is described as having a "90% survival rate," individuals may be more likely to choose it compared to a treatment described as having a "10% mortality rate," even though both descriptions refer to the same information.

Impact of Heuristics and Biases

While heuristics are efficient and often necessary in daily life, cognitive biases that arise from these shortcuts can distort judgment and decision-making. In high-stakes environments such as healthcare or finance, these biases can have serious consequences:

- **In Healthcare:** A doctor might make a quick diagnosis based on the availability heuristic, assuming that a patient's symptoms are similar to those of a previous patient, potentially missing a more serious, but less obvious, condition.
- **In Finance:** An investor might fall prey to confirmation bias by only seeking out positive information about a stock they've already invested in, ignoring signs of potential decline, which could lead to substantial losses.

Mitigating Cognitive Biases

While biases are a natural part of human decision-making, there are strategies to mitigate their effects:

1. **Awareness and Education**: Training individuals to recognize common biases can help them avoid falling into these traps. In healthcare, for example, medical professionals can be trained to recognize and counteract confirmation bias when diagnosing patients.

2. **Structured Decision-Making**: Using structured frameworks or checklists to guide decisions can reduce the influence of biases by encouraging a more thorough and objective evaluation of the situation.

3. **Seeking Diverse Perspectives**: Encouraging collaboration and considering diverse viewpoints can counteract biases such as confirmation bias. In a medical or business setting, consulting colleagues or seeking second opinions can provide alternative perspectives and reduce the likelihood of biased decisions.

4. **Data-Driven Decisions**: Relying on objective data and evidence can help minimize the influence of subjective biases. For instance, in finance, investment decisions based on thorough analysis and data rather than intuition can reduce the impact of biases like overconfidence or anchoring.

4.3 Cognitive Processes in Problem-Solving

Problem-solving involves the application of cognitive resources to find solutions to challenges. Cognitive psychology examines how people approach problems, from simple puzzles to complex, open-ended issues.

Problem-solving is a critical cognitive process that involves the use of mental resources to overcome obstacles and find solutions to challenges. Cognitive psychology explores how individuals approach problems, ranging from simple puzzles to more complex and abstract issues. Understanding how people solve problems helps researchers identify effective strategies and barriers to successful resolution.

Problem-Solving Strategies

Various strategies are employed during problem-solving, and each plays a role in how individuals' approach and resolve challenges. Some of the key strategies include:

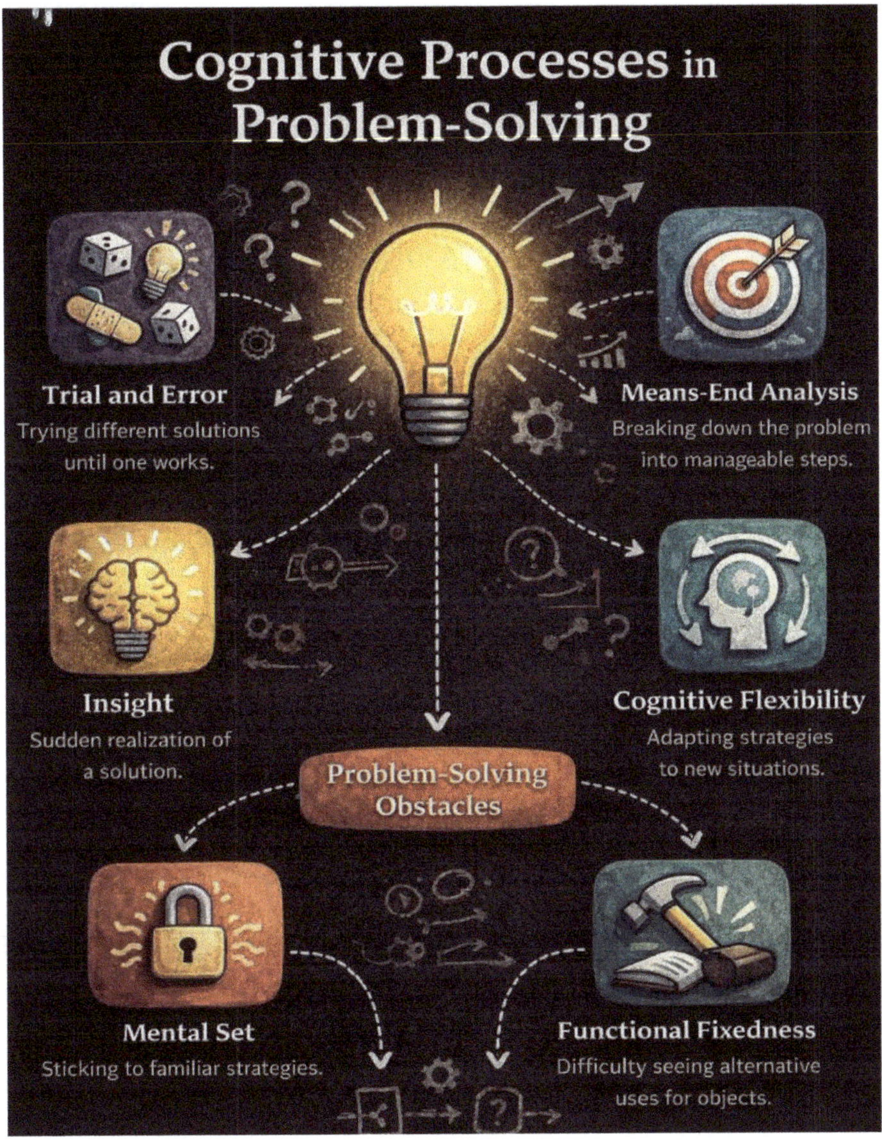

1. Trial and Error :
This is one of the most basic and intuitive methods of problem-solving. In trial and error, individuals attempt different solutions until they find one that works. This strategy is often used when the solution is not immediately clear or when there are few constraints on the potential solutions.

Example: When trying to fix a broken appliance, an individual might try various methods (e.g., unplugging it, checking the connections) until they discover what works to fix the problem.

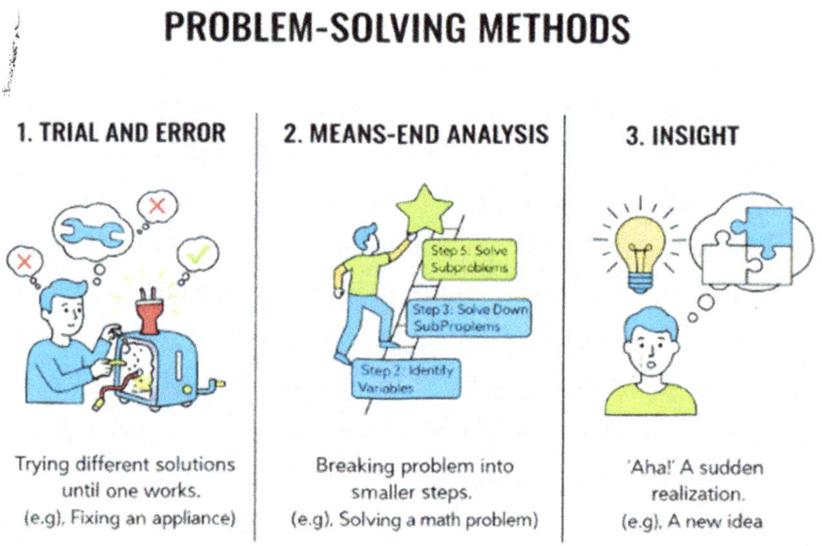

2. Means-End Analysis :
Means-end analysis involves breaking down a complex problem into smaller, more manageable sub-problems. The goal is to reduce the difference between the current state and the desired goal by identifying smaller steps that can be tackled individually. This approach allows people to focus on specific tasks and makes the problem more approachable.

Example: Solving a math problem that involves multiple steps-first, you identify the variables and break down the equation into smaller subproblems (e.g., solving for one variable before the others). Each step progressively brings you closer to the solution.

3. Insight:
Insight refers to the sudden realization of a solution to a problem. It often occurs after a period of contemplation or when the mind shifts its perspective. Unlike step-by-step approaches, insight is a form of "aha moment" where the solution seems to appear almost instantaneously, without the need for conscious effort.

Example: A person trying to solve a word puzzle might suddenly see the correct word after struggling for a while, having experienced a moment of insight or realization.

Cognitive Flexibility

Cognitive flexibility is the ability to adapt one's thinking and strategies to new information or changing circumstances. It is a vital aspect of problem-solving because many problems require a shift in approach when initial strategies fail. Cognitive flexibility allows individuals to reconsider their solutions and try different methods if the current approach isn't working.

Example: In a game of chess, a player might initially plan a strategy based on the pieces on the board but might need to change that strategy if the opponent makes an unexpected move. The ability to adapt and think of a new strategy quickly is an example of cognitive flexibility in action.

Mental Set and Functional Fixedness

While cognitive flexibility aids in problem-solving, **mental set** and **functional fixedness** are cognitive tendencies that can hinder effective problem-solving.

1. Mental Set:
A mental set refers to the tendency to approach problems in a particular way, often based on past experiences or habitual patterns. While this strategy can be useful if it worked before, it can lead to rigid thinking that makes it difficult to consider alternative solutions.

Example: If a person has successfully solved similar puzzles in the past by following a certain method, they may be inclined to repeat that same method, even when it's not suitable for the current problem. This reliance on old strategies can delay finding the correct solution.

2. Functional Fixedness :
Functional fixedness is the tendency to perceive objects and tools only in terms of their usual functions, which can prevent creative problem-solving. It occurs when individuals are unable to see alternative uses for an object or idea, thus limiting their ability to think outside the box.

Example: If a person is trying to fix a broken chair and only considers using a hammer as a tool, they might overlook using a rubber mallet or even a book as a stabilizing base. The inability to think of alternative uses for available tools is an example of functional fixedness.

Implications in Problem-Solving

Problem-solving in real life is influenced by how individuals apply these cognitive strategies, as well as their ability to adapt to new situations. The strategies chosen can depend on the complexity of the problem and the context. However, mental set and functional fixedness can impede progress by causing people to fixate on a single approach or view tools and resources in a limited way. Overcoming these cognitive biases requires conscious effort, and techniques like brainstorming, considering alternative solutions, and engaging in reflective thinking can help improve problem-solving abilities.

Cognitive Style	Analytical Thinking	Intuitive Thinking
Approach to Problems	Logical, structured, and methodical analysis.	Gut feelings, patterns, and quick assessments.
Strengths	- Effective in structured, data-driven environments.	- Useful in uncertain or ambiguous situations.

	- Ensures clarity, precision, and well-reasoned decisions.	- Allows for rapid decision-making.
Decision-Making Process	Breaks down problems into smaller, manageable parts for detailed analysis.	Relies on previous experiences and instincts to arrive at quick decisions.
Best Suited For	- Complex, well-defined problems.	- Dynamic, fast-paced environments.
	- Situations requiring detailed data analysis.	- Ambiguous, time-sensitive challenges.
Challenges	- Can lead to "paralysis by analysis."	- Can result in overconfidence or emotional decisions.
	- Struggles in ambiguous or unclear situations.	- May miss key details or long-term implications.
Example Scenario	Solving a detailed financial analysis problem.	Quickly identifying emerging market trends based on intuition.
Key Focus	Evidence, facts, logical reasoning.	Patterns, feelings, instinctual understanding.

Multiple Choice Questions (MCQs)

1. Which of the following cognitive styles is characterized by using logic, analysis, and structured steps to make decisions?

a) Intuitive thinking
b) Analytical thinking
c) Emotional decision-making
d) Impulsive thinking

Answer: b) Analytical thinking

2. What is a common strength of intuitive thinkers in decision-making?

a) They prefer structured, data-driven approaches.
b) They excel in ambiguous or uncertain situations.
c) They rely heavily on detailed analysis before making decisions.
d) They avoid quick decision-making at all costs.

Answer: b) They excel in ambiguous or uncertain situations.

3. Which problem-solving strategy involves breaking down a complex problem into smaller, more manageable sub-problems?

a) Trial and error
b) Mean-end analysis
c) Insight
d) Availability heuristic

Answer: b) Means-end analysis

4. Which of the following is an example of functional fixedness in problem-solving?

a) Using a hammer to fix a broken chair because you've always used tools in this way.
b) Trying different methods to solve a puzzle until you find the right solution.
c) Quickly recognizing a solution to a problem through an intuitive insight.
d) Breaking down a complex task into smaller steps to handle it more easily.

Answer: a) Using a hammer to fix a broken chair because you've always used tools in this way.

5. What cognitive bias occurs when individuals Favor information that confirms their pre-existing beliefs or assumptions?

a) Anchoring bias
b) Confirmation bias
c) Availability bias
d) Framing effect

Answer: b) Confirmation bias

Short Answer Questions

1. What is the difference between analytical and intuitive thinking in decision-making?
2. Explain the concept of "means-end analysis" in problem-solving.
3. How does cognitive flexibility enhance the decision-making process?
4. What is functional fixedness, and how can it hinder problem-solving?
5. How does confirmation bias affect decision-making?
6. Why is insight considered a unique form of problem-solving?

Long Answer Questions

1. Discuss the strengths and challenges associated with both analytical and intuitive thinking in decision-making. Provide examples of when each style would be more effective.
2. Describe the role of cognitive biases like anchoring bias and confirmation bias in decision-making.

3. Explain the importance of problem-solving strategies such as trial and error, means-end analysis, and insight. How do these strategies differ in their approach to finding solutions?

4. Examine the concept of cognitive flexibility and its role in problem-solving. How does the ability to shift between different strategies improve outcomes in dynamic environments?

5. What is the relationship between mental set and problem-solving? How can mental set lead to errors in judgment, and what strategies can be used to overcome this barrier?

6. Analyse how cognitive styles and biases affect decision-making in a professional setting.

5

The Role of Emotion in Cognition

5.1 The Interaction Between Emotion and Thought

Emotion and cognition are intricately connected, influencing each other in complex ways. Emotional states can shape cognitive processes such as memory, attention, and decision-making.

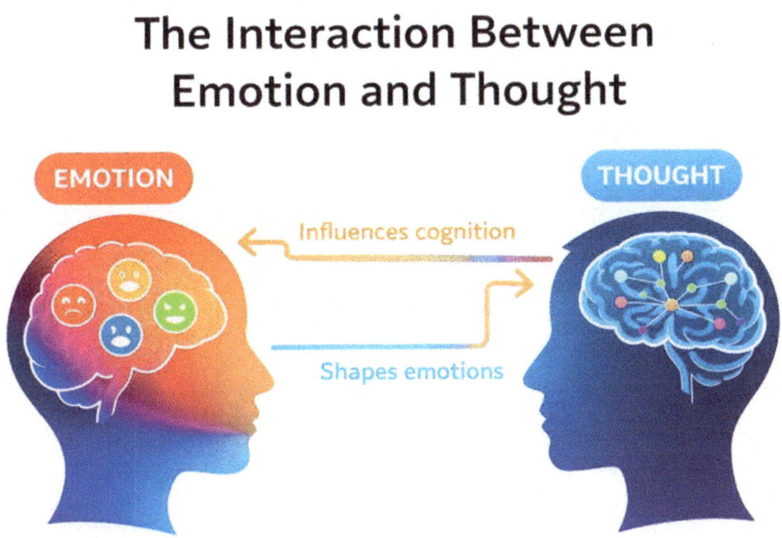

Emotion and cognition are deeply intertwined, constantly influencing one another in ways that affect our thoughts and behaviours. Emotions can have a significant impact on cognitive functions such as memory, attention, and decision-making. For example, a person experiencing anxiety might have a more limited focus, concentrating on the source of the anxiety and disregarding other important details. This narrow focus can impair judgment and hinder rational decision-making. On the other hand, positive emotions, like happiness or excitement, can enhance cognitive abilities, fostering creativity and improving problem-solving skills by expanding the individual's thought processes.

Conversely, cognition-how we think about and interpret events-can shape our emotional experiences. For instance, how a person perceives a challenging situation can determine their emotional response. If someone interprets a stressful event as a challenge, they may feel motivated to rise to the occasion, whereas interpreting it as a threat could lead to feelings of fear or helplessness. This reciprocal relationship between emotion and cognition suggests that our emotional states are not just reactive but also actively shape the way we think.

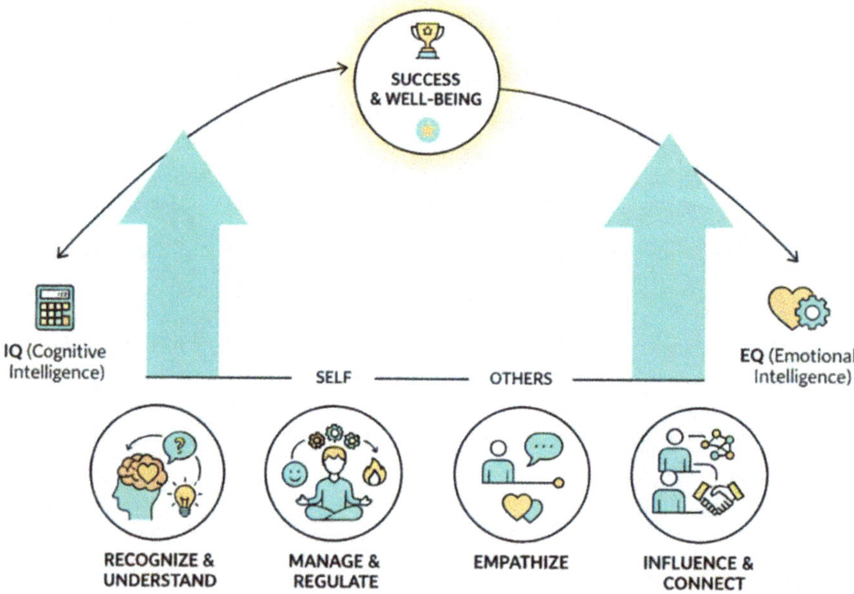

The complex interplay between emotion and thought is essential to understanding human behaviour, especially in fields like psychology, marketing, and therapy. In psychology, it can help explain mood disorders or the effects of emotional regulation on cognitive performance. In marketing, understanding how emotions influence decision-making can aid in creating persuasive advertisements or campaigns. In therapy, recognizing how emotional states affect cognition allows for more effective interventions, such as cognitive-behavioural therapy, which works to alter both thoughts and emotional responses. This bidirectional interaction underscores the significant role that emotions play in shaping our overall cognitive experiences.

5.2 Emotional Intelligence

Emotional intelligence (EI) refers to the ability to recognize, understand, manage, and influence emotions in oneself and others. Research by Daniel Goleman suggests that EI is as important as cognitive intelligence (IQ) for personal and professional success.

Emotional intelligence (EI) is the ability to recognize, understand, manage, and influence emotions in both oneself and others. According to Daniel Goleman's research, EI is just as important as cognitive intelligence (IQ) for achieving success in both personal and professional contexts. People with high EI are adept at recognizing their emotions and controlling their reactions, which allows them to effectively handle stress and navigate complex social interactions. They are also skilled at empathizing with others, understanding their emotions, and responding appropriately.

One of the key aspects of EI is emotional regulation, which involves managing emotional responses, especially in challenging situations. High EI individuals can remain calm under pressure, reducing the likelihood of impulsive decisions that could lead to negative outcomes. They also tend to have better social relationships, as they can navigate conflicts with more tact and understanding, fostering stronger connections with others.

EI significantly impacts decision-making processes. People with high EI are able to balance their emotions and rational thinking, allowing them to make more thoughtful and deliberate decisions. In leadership, EI plays a vital role as leaders with high EI can motivate and inspire their teams, build trust, and effectively manage diverse groups of people.

Training emotional intelligence skills can enhance cognitive performance by improving self-awareness, self-regulation, empathy, and social skills. These skills contribute to healthier interpersonal dynamics, making it easier to resolve conflicts, collaborate effectively, and solve problems. As a result, individuals with higher EI tend to excel in areas such as teamwork, communication, and conflict resolution, which are essential for personal growth and professional achievement.

5.3 The Neurobiology of Emotions

The brain structures involved in emotional processing, such as the amygdala, prefrontal cortex, and hippocampus, play a crucial role in how emotions influence cognition. The amygdala processes emotional responses, particularly fear, while the prefrontal cortex helps regulate these emotions and guide appropriate behaviour.

The neurobiology of emotions delves into how various brain structures influence and regulate emotional experiences and responses. Key areas involved in emotional processing include the **amygdala**, **prefrontal cortex**, and **hippocampus**, each playing a distinct but interconnected role in how emotions impact cognition.

1. **Amygdala**: The amygdala is central to the processing of emotions, particularly fear and other negative emotions. It detects emotional stimuli and triggers an appropriate emotional response. The amygdala plays a vital role in the fight-or-flight response, alerting the body to potential threats. In situations of high stress or danger, the amygdala can activate physiological reactions, such as increased heart rate and heightened awareness, to prepare the body for quick action.

2. **Prefrontal Cortex**: While the amygdala triggers emotional responses, the **prefrontal cortex** is responsible for regulating these emotions. It helps modulate impulsive behaviours, enabling more thoughtful decision-making and appropriate emotional responses. The prefrontal cortex is involved in **executive functions**, such as planning, reasoning, and controlling emotional reactions. When functioning well, it can help us manage fear, anger, or anxiety by guiding us to respond rationally rather than react impulsively.

3. **Hippocampus** : The hippocampus plays a key role in **memory formation** and the integration of emotional experiences. It helps store emotional memories, allowing us to learn from past experiences. The hippocampus interacts with the amygdala, linking emotional responses to contextual memories. For instance, if a person has previously encountered a stressful situation, the hippocampus can help trigger a similar emotional response when faced with a comparable event in the future.

Neuroplasticity and Emotional Experience :
Research has shown that **emotional experiences** can reshape brain activity and structure. For example, long-term emotional exposure can strengthen certain **neural pathways** related to emotional memory and judgment. If someone repeatedly experiences stress, the neural circuits involved in processing fear and anxiety may become more pronounced, leading to heightened sensitivity to stress. This neuroplasticity highlights the brain's ability to adapt and reorganize in response to emotional experiences.

Implications for Mental Health :
Understanding the neurobiology of emotions provides crucial insight into emotional disorders such as **depression** and **anxiety**. In conditions like these, the normal regulation of emotions by the prefrontal cortex may be impaired, while the amygdala's response to fear or stress might be exaggerated. This imbalance can contribute to heightened emotional responses, poor coping mechanisms, and difficulties in emotional regulation.

For instance, in anxiety disorders, the amygdala may become overactive, leading to heightened fear responses, while the prefrontal cortex may struggle to regulate these feelings appropriately. Similarly, in depression, there may be an altered interaction between the hippocampus and amygdala, influencing the processing of memories and emotional regulation, which can lead to persistent negative emotions and distorted thinking.

This neurobiological perspective emphasizes the complex physiological underpinnings of how emotion and cognition interact, offering insights into how disorders arise and providing a foundation for treatments such as

cognitive-behavioural therapy (CBT), which helps retrain the brain to regulate emotional responses more effectively.

5.4 Emotion Regulation and Cognitive Control

Emotion regulation refers to the strategies people use to influence their emotional experiences, such as reappraisal (changing the way one thinks about a situation) or suppression (inhibiting emotional expression).

Emotion regulation refers to the strategies individuals use to influence their emotional experiences, either by changing the way they feel about a situation or by managing their emotional responses. These strategies are crucial for maintaining **cognitive control**-the ability to focus attention, suppress impulsive reactions, and think clearly, especially in challenging or emotional situations.

Two common strategies of emotion regulation are:

1. **Reappraisal**: This involves changing the way a person interprets or thinks about a situation to alter its emotional impact. For example, if someone feels anxious about a presentation, they might reframe the experience by viewing it as an opportunity to showcase their skills rather than as a threat.

2. **Suppression**: Suppression involves inhibiting the outward expression of emotions. While it may involve hiding emotions like anger or sadness, it doesn't necessarily change the internal emotional experience. For instance, someone might choose not to express frustration during a meeting even though they feel irritated.

Effective Emotion Regulation and Cognitive Control:
When individuals successfully regulate their emotions, they can maintain cognitive control, allowing them to remain focused, think logically, and make sound decisions even under stress. This is especially important in situations where quick, rational thinking is needed, such as in high-pressure work environments or when making important life decisions.

For instance, an individual with strong emotion regulation might be able to remain calm and composed during an argument, allowing them to think through their responses thoughtfully instead of reacting impulsively. By managing their emotional responses, they can maintain focus and respond more effectively to the situation.

The Relationship Between Emotion Regulation and Cognitive Control : Cognitive control involves overriding automatic responses or impulses. Emotion regulation plays a significant role in this process. When an individual experiences strong emotions, such as anger or fear, they may feel an automatic urge to act impulsively. However, by effectively regulating emotions, a person can prevent these impulses from dictating their actions, allowing them to act more rationally and in line with their goals.

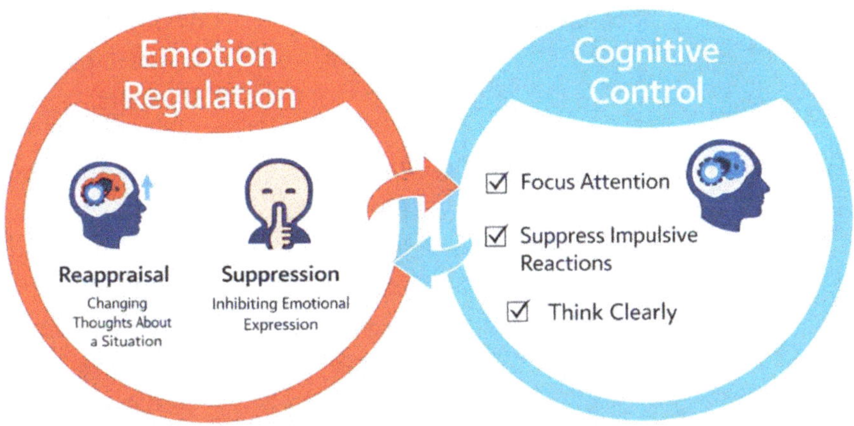

Effective Emotion Regulation Helps Maintain Cognitive Control

Both emotion regulation and cognitive control are essential for **mental health** and overall **well-being**. Poor emotion regulation can lead to difficulties in controlling emotions, which may contribute to mental health issues like **anxiety**, **depression**, or **anger management problems** . On the other hand, effective emotion regulation contributes to better self-discipline, increased resilience in the face of stress, and improved relationships.

Brain Structure	Role in Emotional Processing	Associated Functions	Implications for Mental Health
Amygdala	Processes emotional responses, especially fear and threat.	Detects emotional stimuli, triggers fight-or-flight response.	Overactivity linked to anxiety, fear disorders, and PTSD.
Prefrontal Cortex	Regulates emotions and guides appropriate behaviour.	Executive functions like decision-making, impulse control.	Impaired regulation linked to impulsivity, emotional dysregulation (e.g., in ADHD or mood disorders).
Hippocampus	Stores and integrates emotional memories and experiences.	Memory formation, linking emotional responses to past events.	Altered functioning linked to PTSD, depression, and anxiety, affecting emotional memory processing.
Neuroplasticity	Strengthens or weakens neural pathways in response to emotion.	Enhances emotional memory, judgment, and decision-making.	Chronic stress and negative emotions can reinforce pathways related to anxiety and depression.

Multiple Choice Questions (MCQs)

1. Which brain structure is primarily responsible for processing emotional responses, particularly fear?

A) Prefrontal Cortex
B) Hippocampus
C) Amygdala
D) Cerebellum

Answer: C) Amygdala

2. Emotional intelligence (EI) is important for which of the following?

A) Maintaining cognitive control and making reasoned decisions
B) Enhancing memory retrieval in stressful situations
C) Lowering emotional reactivity in non-stressful situations
D) Decreasing brain activity in the prefrontal cortex

Answer: A) Maintaining cognitive control and making reasoned decisions

3. Which emotion regulation strategy involves changing the way one thinks about a situation to alter its emotional impact?

A) Suppression
B) Reappraisal
C) Denial
D) Emotional Blunting

Answer: B) Reappraisal

4. Cognitive control is best defined as the ability to:

A) Suppress emotional responses completely
B) Override automatic impulses and responses
C) Process emotions faster than thoughts
D) Ignore emotional memories during decision-making

Answer: B) Override automatic impulses and responses

5. The interaction between emotion and cognition suggests that:

A) Emotions only affect physical health, not cognitive functions.
B) Emotional experiences can alter brain activity and strengthen emotional memories.
C) Cognitive processes inhibit all emotional responses.
D) Emotions have no impact on decision-making processes.

Answer: B) Emotional experiences can alter brain activity and strengthen emotional memories.

Short Answer Questions

1. What role does the amygdala play in emotional processing?
2. How does emotional intelligence (EI) impact decision-making?
3. What is the difference between reappraisal and suppression as emotion regulation strategies?
4. Explain the relationship between emotion regulation and cognitive control.
5. How does emotional experience influence memory formation?
6. What are the consequences of impaired emotional regulation on mental health?

Long Answer Questions

1. Discuss the neurobiological mechanisms behind the processing of emotions, including the roles of the amygdala, prefrontal cortex, and hippocampus.
2. In what ways does emotional intelligence (EI) contribute to professional success?

3. Explain the concept of emotional regulation. How do strategies like reappraisal and suppression affect an individual's ability to manage stress and make decisions in emotionally charged situations?

4. Describe how cognitive control is related to emotion regulation. Discuss how the ability to regulate emotions helps in overriding automatic responses and making reasoned decisions.

5. How does the interaction between emotion and cognition affect mental health disorders such as depression and anxiety? Provide insights into how these disorders may be linked to disruptions in emotional regulation and cognitive processes.

6. Explore the role of emotion in decision-making. How can emotions influence the judgment process, and how does effective emotion regulation help improve decision-making in both personal and professional contexts?

6

Cognitive Development Across the Lifespan

6.1 Theories of Cognitive Development

Cognitive development refers to how thinking and understanding evolve over a person's life. Prominent theories of cognitive development include Jean Piaget's stage theory, which outlines how children move through distinct stages of cognitive abilities, from sensory-motor to formal operations.

Cognitive development refers to the process through which individuals grow and change in their mental capacities, such as thinking, understanding, problem-solving, and decision-making, throughout their life. Various theories have been proposed to explain this complex process, with some of the most influential being those of Jean Piaget, Lev Vygotsky, and Erik Erikson.

Jean Piaget's Stage Theory : Piaget is well-known for his theory of cognitive development, which outlines distinct stages through which children pass as they grow. He identified four key stages: the sensorimotor stage (birth to 2 years), the preoperational stage (2 to 7 years), the concrete operational stage (7 to 11 years), and the formal operational stage (12 years and beyond). According to Piaget, children move through these stages in a fixed order, and each stage represents a different way of thinking and understanding the world around them. For example, during the sensorimotor stage, infants develop object permanence-the understanding that objects continue to exist even when they cannot be seen. In contrast, the formal operational stage is marked by the ability to think abstractly and hypothetically.

Lev Vygotsky's Sociocultural Theory : Vygotsky emphasized the role of social interaction and culture in cognitive development. Unlike Piaget, who believed that cognitive development was largely driven by internal factors, Vygotsky argued that learning is deeply influenced by the social environment and cultural context. He introduced the concept of the Zone of Proximal Development (ZPD), which refers to the difference between what a child can do independently and what they can do with the help of more knowledgeable others, such as teachers or peers. Vygotsky's theory highlights the importance of social interaction, language, and collaborative learning in fostering cognitive growth.

Erik Erikson's Psychosocial Stages : While primarily known for his work on psychosocial development, Erikson's theory also has implications for cognitive growth. He proposed eight stages of development, each characterized by a central conflict. As individuals move through these stages, they encounter challenges that influence their cognitive and emotional growth. For example, in adolescence, the conflict between identity and role confusion plays a critical role in shaping how young people think about themselves and their place in the world. Erikson's theory suggests that cognitive development cannot be separated from emotional and social development, and that individuals grow cognitively as they navigate various social and emotional challenges.

6.2 Cognitive Growth in Childhood

During childhood, significant cognitive milestones are achieved. Early in life, infants develop object permanence, understanding that objects continue to exist even when not seen.

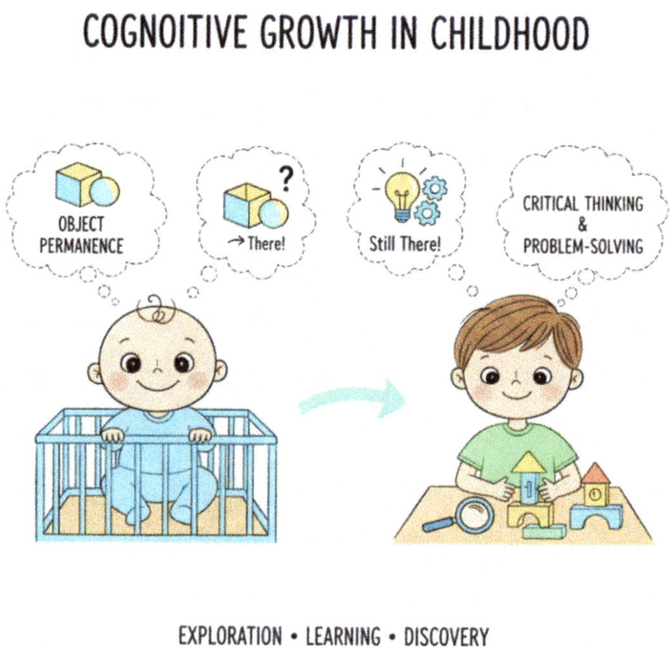

Cognitive growth during childhood involves a series of significant milestones that contribute to a child's understanding of the world and their ability to interact with it effectively. From infancy through early adolescence, children experience profound cognitive changes that enable them to think, reason, and solve problems in increasingly complex ways.

Object Permanence : One of the first major cognitive milestones in infancy is the development of object permanence. This refers to the understanding that objects continue to exist even when they are not visible. In the early months of life, infants are not aware that objects exist outside of their direct perception. However, as they grow, they begin to recognize that objects, people, and events continue to exist even when out of sight. This is a fundamental aspect of cognitive development, as it shows the beginnings of mental representation and memory.

Symbolic Thinking and Imaginative Play : As children enter the toddler and preschool years, they begin to engage in symbolic thinking, which allows them to use objects or actions to represent other things. This is most evident in imaginative or pretend play, where children create and enact scenarios using toys, language, and gestures. Symbolic thinking is crucial for the development of language, problem-solving skills, and the ability to understand abstract concepts. For example, a child may use a stick as a pretend sword or imagine that a box is a house, demonstrating an ability to manipulate ideas and objects in the mind.

Concrete Operational Stage : As children enter the middle childhood years, typically around age 7, they move into Piaget's concrete operational stage. During this stage, children develop the ability to think logically about concrete events and objects. They can now understand concepts like conservation (the idea that quantity remains the same despite changes in shape or appearance) and reversibility (the ability to recognize that objects or numbers can be changed and then returned to their original state). Their thinking becomes more systematic, but it is still tied to tangible experiences and objects. For instance, children can solve math problems or categorize objects based on specific attributes, but they still struggle with abstract or hypothetical reasoning.

Language Acquisition : Language development is another critical aspect of cognitive growth during childhood. From birth, children begin acquiring language skills, influenced by both genetic predispositions and environmental factors. Early language development includes recognizing sounds, forming basic words, and eventually stringing words into sentences. As children grow, their vocabulary expands, and they gain a better understanding of grammar and syntax. Language acquisition supports cognitive growth by enabling children to express thoughts, ask questions, and engage in more complex forms of social interaction. The rich social interactions children have with their caregivers, peers, and teachers play a vital role in shaping their language skills.

Memory, Attention, and Problem-Solving : Cognitive psychology also focuses on how children develop memory, attention, and problem-solving abilities. As children age, their capacity for attention increases, allowing them to focus on tasks for longer periods and process more information at once. Memory improves as well, with children gradually transitioning from simple recall of facts to more sophisticated strategies for organizing and retrieving information. Problem-solving abilities also become more advanced, with children learning to approach challenges in more structured and creative ways. For example, they may learn to break down a task into

6.3 Adolescence and Cognitive Changes

Adolescence is marked by significant cognitive changes as the brain matures and becomes capable of abstract thought. During this stage, individuals develop the ability to think hypothetically and engage in advanced problem-solving and reasoning.

Adolescence is a period of rapid cognitive development, marked by profound changes in how individuals think, reason, and understand the world. As the brain matures, adolescents gain the ability to engage in more sophisticated cognitive tasks, though this development is not uniform across all areas. Adolescence is a time when cognitive abilities expand to include abstract thought, complex reasoning, and the exploration of identity.

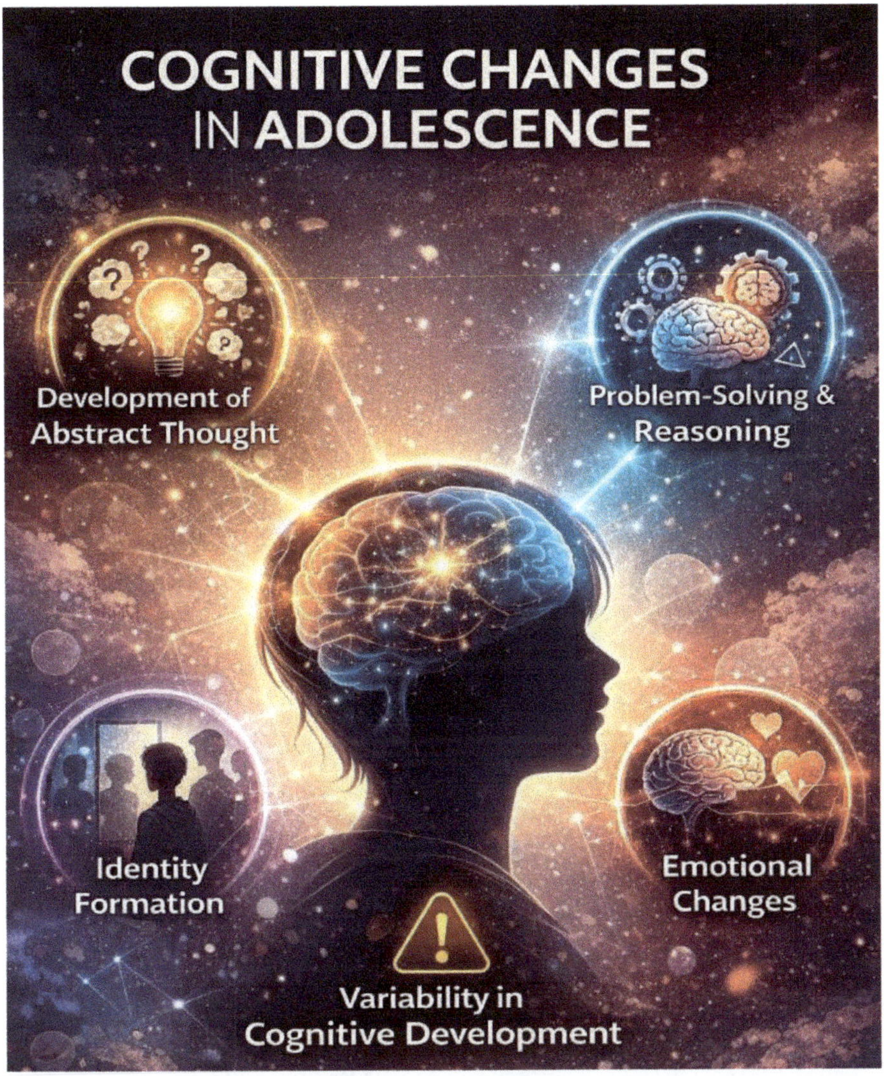

Development of Abstract Thought : One of the key cognitive changes during adolescence is the transition from concrete thinking (focused on tangible, real-world situations) to abstract thinking (which involves considering hypothetical scenarios and abstract concepts).

This change, as described by Piaget in his formal operational stage, allows adolescents to think beyond their immediate experiences and begin considering possibilities, future outcomes, and moral dilemmas. For example, adolescents can think about hypothetical situations, such as "What would happen if everyone stopped going to school?" or engage in debates about ethical issues like justice or rights. This newfound capacity for abstract thought plays a critical role in intellectual development and allows adolescents to engage with more complex ideas and concepts.

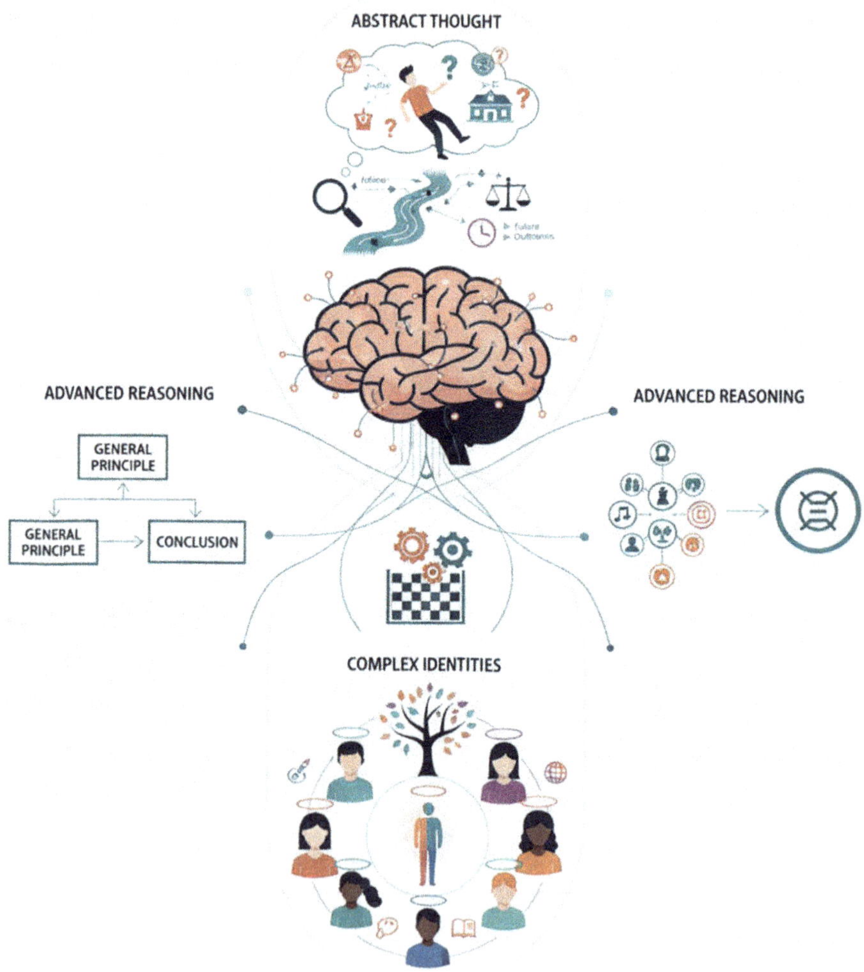

Advanced Problem-Solving and Reasoning : As adolescents mature, they develop more sophisticated problem-solving skills and are better able to analyse complex situations. This includes the ability to consider multiple variables at once, weigh evidence, and apply logic to unfamiliar problems. In contrast to younger children, who tend to use trial and error or rely on simpler solutions, adolescents can approach problems in a more systematic and analytical way. They also begin to engage in deductive reasoning, where they can make conclusions based on general principles or theories, and inductive reasoning, where they generalize from specific observations to broader conclusions.

Formation of Complex Identities : Cognitive development in adolescence is closely tied to the formation of a more complex sense of self and identity. As adolescents gain the ability to think abstractly, they also begin to reflect on their personal values, goals, and beliefs. This period is often marked by exploration of different roles and identities, influenced by social interactions, culture, and individual experiences. Adolescents may experiment with different ways of thinking, behaving, and interacting with others as they seek to understand who they are and where they fit into the world. This cognitive process of identity formation is not only about intellectual development but also about emotional and social growth.

Variability in Cognitive Development : Although adolescence is generally characterized by advances in cognitive abilities, cognitive development does not occur uniformly. Some adolescents may excel in abstract reasoning and problem-solving, while others may struggle with impulsive behaviour, poor decision-making, and difficulty with impulse control. The brain's prefrontal cortex, responsible for executive functions such as planning, impulse control, and decision-making, is still maturing during adolescence, which can result in a mismatch between cognitive potential and emotional regulation. For instance, while adolescents may be capable of thinking abstractly and logically, they may also be prone to risky behaviours and poor judgment due to underdeveloped impulse control and the influence of emotional factors.

Cognitive and Emotional Changes : The cognitive and emotional changes that occur during adolescence are deeply interconnected. As adolescents develop the ability to think more abstractly, they also become more aware of their emotions and how these emotions influence their thinking and behaviour. This heightened emotional awareness can lead to greater self-consciousness and sensitivity to social feedback. Additionally, the increased emotional intensity experienced during adolescence, often linked to changes in brain chemistry and hormonal fluctuations, can impact cognitive processes like decision-making and social reasoning. For example, adolescents may be more likely to make decisions based on emotional reactions rather than logical analysis, especially in social situations or under stress.

Multiple Choice Questions (MCQs)

1. At what stage of cognitive development, according to Jean Piaget, do children begin to think logically about concrete events?

a) Sensorimotor
b) Preoperational
c) Concrete operational
d) Formal operational

Answer: c) Concrete operational

2. Which of the following abilities typically declines with age?

a) Vocabulary
b) Crystallized intelligence
c) Working memory
d) Accumulated knowledge

Answer: c) Working memory

3. According to Lev Vygotsky's theory, what plays a crucial role in cognitive development?

a) Self-regulation
b) Physical activity
c) Social interaction and cultural context
d) Biological maturation

Answer: c) Social interaction and cultural context

4. Which of the following is an example of a cognitive change that occurs during adolescence?

a) Increase in crystallized intelligence
b) Development of abstract thinking
c) Decrease in processing speed
d) Decline in long-term memory

Answer: b) Development of abstract thinking

5. In cognitive aging, which of the following typically remains stable or improves with age?

a) Fluid intelligence
b) Processing speed
c) Vocabulary
d) Working memory

Answer: c) Vocabulary

Short Answer Questions

1. What is the key characteristic of the sensorimotor stage of cognitive development?
2. How does Vygotsky's concept of the Zone of Proximal Development contribute to understanding cognitive development?
3. What cognitive abilities typically decline with age, and why?
4. Explain the difference between fluid and crystallized intelligence.
5. What role does language acquisition play in cognitive development during childhood?
6. How does the development of abstract thinking in adolescence influence problem-solving abilities?

Long Answer Questions

1. Discuss the stages of cognitive development according to Jean Piaget, explaining the key characteristics of each stage and how children's thinking evolves as they move through them.

2. Explain the impact of social interaction and cultural context on cognitive development, according to Lev Vygotsky. How does his theory differ from Piaget's approach to cognitive development?

3. Describe the cognitive changes that typically occur during adolescence, and explain how these changes support the development of advanced problem-solving and reasoning skills.

4. Examine the relationship between cognitive aging and the decline in processing speed and working memory, and discuss strategies that can help mitigate these effects.

5. What are the differences in cognitive development between childhood and adulthood, specifically regarding memory, attention, and problem-solving abilities?

6. In the context of cognitive aging, how do conditions like Alzheimer's disease and dementia influence cognitive functions such as memory and reasoning?

7

Social Cognition: Understanding Others and Ourselves

7.1 Social Perception and Attribution

Social perception refers to the process through which we form impressions of others and interpret their behaviour. Cognitive psychologists study how individuals perceive social cues, such as facial expressions, body language, and tone of voice, to understand others' emotions and intentions.

Social perception is the process by which we form judgments and impressions about others, based on the information we receive through social cues such as facial expressions, body language, and tone of voice. This process helps us understand the emotions, intentions, and motivations of those around us. For example, when someone smiles or maintains eye contact, we may interpret these cues as signs of friendliness or confidence. Conversely, crossed arms or averted gaze might signal defensiveness or discomfort. These interpretations are vital for effective communication and building relationships, as they guide our reactions and behaviours in social contexts.

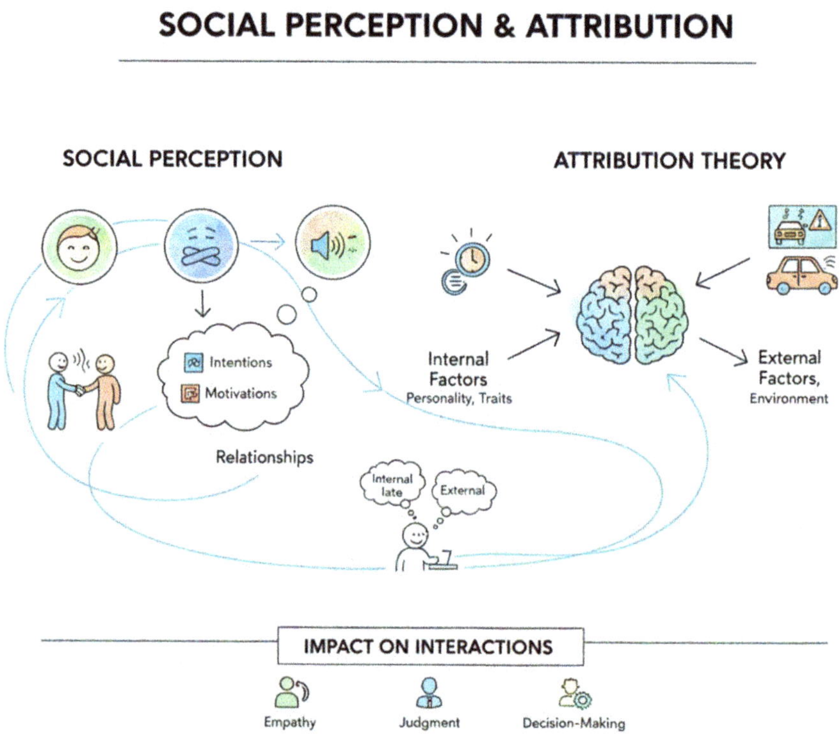

Attribution theory, developed by psychologist Fritz Heider, explains how individuals make sense of the causes behind others' actions. It suggests that people tend to attribute behaviours to either internal or external factors. Internal attributions are made when we believe a person's actions are due to their inherent traits or personality. For instance, if a colleague is late to a meeting, we might attribute this to their lack of punctuality or laziness. External attributions, on the other hand, occur when we believe that external circumstances or factors are responsible for the behaviour. In the same scenario, we might attribute the colleague's tardiness to unexpected traffic or a prior meeting running late.

These attribution processes play a significant role in social interactions. They influence how we evaluate and respond to others, affecting our relationships, judgment, and decision-making. For example, if we consistently make internal attributions for others' mistakes, it may lead to negative perceptions and strained relationships. Conversely, if we are more likely to consider external factors, we might develop a more empathetic understanding of others' behaviours. Thus, the way we perceive and attribute social behaviour shapes our attitudes, interactions, and overall social dynamics.

7.2 The Self and Identity

The concept of self is central to social cognition, and self-identity involves the way individuals perceive and define themselves. Cognitive psychologists study how people form their self-concept based on internal thoughts and external feedback.

The concept of self is fundamental to social cognition, as it refers to how individuals perceive and define themselves. This self-concept is not fixed; rather, it evolves over time through a complex interplay of internal reflections and external feedback. Cognitive psychologists study this process to understand how people form their sense of identity, examining the ways in which our thoughts, experiences, and social interactions shape who we believe we are.

A key theory in understanding self-identity is **Social Identity Theory**, proposed by Henri Tajfel. According to this theory, a significant portion of our self-identity is derived from the social groups we belong to. These groups could include familial ties, ethnic backgrounds, religious affiliations, and professional roles. The groups we associate with not only influence how we view ourselves but also how we relate to others. For example, a person may feel a strong sense of pride and belonging in their ethnic group, which may shape their social interactions and even their views on cultural issues.

Case studies exploring ethnic identity in multicultural societies provide vivid examples of how group membership affects self-identity and individual behaviour. In diverse societies, individuals often navigate between multiple group identities, such as national, religious, or ethnic identities. These overlapping identities can impact behaviour, attitudes, and social interactions, as individuals may adjust their self-concept based on the norms and expectations of the various groups they belong to. In multicultural societies, ethnic identity is often central to how people define themselves, influencing everything from personal pride to social integration and even political engagement.

The formation of self-identity is a dynamic and ongoing process, shaped by personal experiences, social interactions, and societal expectations. As individuals interact with others, they receive feedback that can affirm or challenge their sense of self. Additionally, external factors like societal norms, cultural values, and media representations play a crucial role in shaping how people see themselves and how they are seen by others. Thus, self-identity is not only a personal construct but also a social one, constantly evolving as individuals engage with the world around them.

7.3 Stereotypes, Prejudices, and Discrimination

Stereotyping involves generalizing traits to a group of people based on their membership in a particular category, such as gender, race, or age. These cognitive shortcuts can lead to prejudices, or negative attitudes, and discrimination, which involves treating people unfairly based on stereotypes.

Stereotyping refers to the cognitive process of attributing certain characteristics or traits to a group of people based on their membership in a specific category, such as gender, race, age, or social class. These generalizations, while sometimes based on limited information, serve as cognitive shortcuts that help individuals process complex social information more quickly. However, stereotypes often oversimplify and exaggerate differences between groups, leading to skewed perceptions and inaccurate judgments. For example, associating certain personality traits with individuals from a particular ethnic group may lead to misunderstanding or misjudging people based on superficial characteristics rather than their individual qualities.

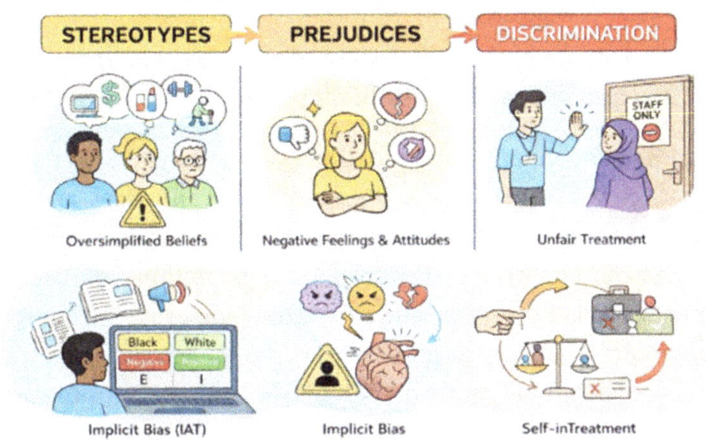

Stereotyping can give rise to **prejudices**, which are negative attitudes or beliefs directed towards individuals based on their membership in a particular group. These prejudices can manifest in various forms, such as racism, sexism, ageism, or homophobia. Prejudiced attitudes are often rooted in stereotypes and may result in discriminatory behaviour, which involves treating people unfairly or unjustly because of their group membership. Discrimination can take many forms, from overt actions like verbal abuse or exclusion to more subtle forms, such as unequal opportunities or biased decision-making in professional or social settings.

Cognitive psychologists have studied the mechanisms behind stereotyping to understand how and why these mental shortcuts are formed and maintained. Research has shown that stereotypes can be deeply ingrained in our thinking, often being influenced by socialization, cultural narratives, and media representations. Additionally, once formed, stereotypes can become self-reinforcing. For example, individuals may notice behaviours that confirm their existing stereotypes and ignore behaviours that contradict them, leading to the perpetuation of biased views over time.

One widely used tool to measure implicit biases is the **Implicit Association Test (IAT)**. The IAT measures automatic associations between categories (such as race or gender) and positive or negative traits. For instance, an individual may implicitly associate certain racial groups with negative attributes, even if they consciously reject such beliefs. This highlights the automatic and often unconscious nature of prejudice, making it difficult for individuals to recognize and address their biases.

Understanding the cognitive foundations of stereotypes, prejudices, and discrimination is essential for addressing social injustices and fostering inclusivity. By recognizing how these biases form and influence behaviour, it becomes possible to develop strategies for reducing their impact, such as through education, awareness, and promoting empathy. Encouraging self-reflection and creating environments that challenge stereotypes can help individuals become more aware of their biases and take steps towards more equitable interactions.

7.4 Empathy and Theory of Mind

Empathy refers to the ability to understand and share the feelings of others, while theory of mind (ToM) is the cognitive ability to attribute mental states, such as beliefs and intentions, to oneself and others.

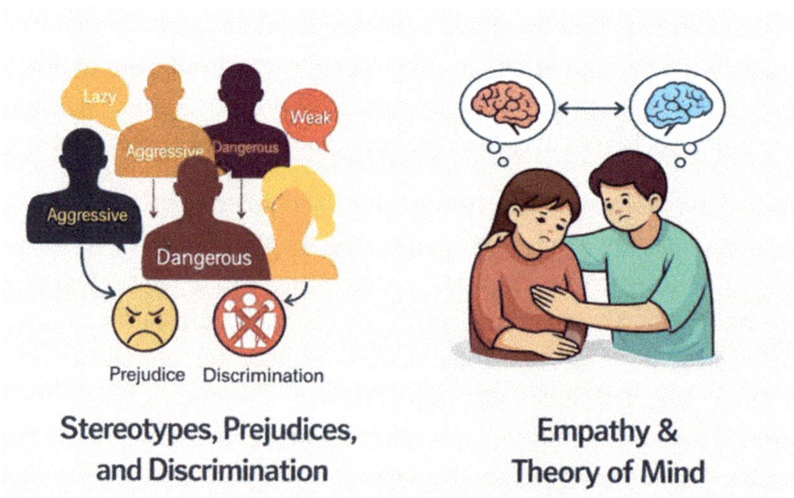

Empathy is the capacity to recognize, understand, and share the feelings of others. It involves both cognitive and emotional components-cognitive empathy is the ability to understand what someone else is feeling, while emotional empathy refers to actually experiencing a similar emotion. For instance, when someone feels sadness due to a loss, empathy allows us to not only comprehend their sorrow but also to emotionally connect with that experience. Empathy plays a critical role in fostering social bonds, as it motivates compassionate actions, promotes prosocial behaviour, and strengthens interpersonal relationships. In both personal and professional contexts, empathy is vital for cooperation, conflict resolution, and maintaining healthy connections with others.

Theory of Mind (ToM) refers to the cognitive ability to attribute mental states-such as beliefs, desires, intentions, and knowledge-to oneself and others, recognizing that others can have beliefs and perspectives different from one's own. ToM is essential for navigating social interactions, as it allows individuals to understand and predict others' behaviour based on their internal states. The development of ToM is considered a crucial milestone in childhood cognitive growth, as it marks the beginning of more sophisticated social engagement.

A classic experiment used to test **Theory of Mind** in children is the **"false-belief task"**. In this task, a child is shown a scenario in which one-character places an object in a box and leaves the room. Another character moves the object to a different location. The child is then asked where the first character will look for the object upon returning. Children who have developed ToM understand that the character will look in the original location, as that is where the character believes the object to be, even though the child knows the object has been moved. This ability to recognize that others can hold beliefs about the world that are different from reality is a fundamental aspect of social understanding and helps facilitate more complex interactions.

Both empathy and ToM are crucial for effective communication and problem-solving in social settings. They enable individuals to consider the perspectives and emotions of others, leading to more collaborative behaviours and the ability to manage disagreements constructively. In professional environments, these skills contribute to leadership, teamwork, and customer relations, helping to build trust and ensure that interactions are more understanding and considerate.

Multiple Choice Questions (MCQs)

1. What is social perception primarily concerned with?

A) Understanding emotions
B) Making judgments about others based on social cues
C) Understanding personal beliefs
D) Developing interpersonal communication skills

Answer: B) Making judgments about others based on social cues

2. According to Attribution Theory, internal attributions are:

A) Attributed to external factors, like the situation
B) Made when behaviour is attributed to a person's inherent traits or characteristics
C) Made when behaviour is due to uncontrollable factors
D) Always negative

Answer: B) Made when behaviour is attributed to a person's inherent traits or characteristics

3. Social Identity Theory suggests that:

A) Self-identity is formed only through personal achievements
B) People identify solely with their professional groups
C) People derive part of their self-concept from group memberships
D) Group memberships do not influence individual behaviour

Answer: C) People derive part of their self-concept from group memberships

4. Which of the following best describes the false-belief task in the context of Theory of Mind?

A) Understanding that children cannot hold beliefs different from reality

B) Recognizing that others can have beliefs that differ from reality
C) Understanding one's own beliefs and intentions
D) Knowing how to manipulate others' beliefs

Answer: B) Recognizing that others can have beliefs that differ from reality

5. Empathy involves:

A) Only understanding another person's feelings
B) Both understanding and sharing another person's emotions
C) Refraining from emotional engagement with others
D) Ignoring others' emotions to avoid conflict

Answer: B) Both understanding and sharing another person's emotions

Short Answer Questions

1. What is the main focus of social perception in social cognition?
2. How do internal and external attributions differ according to Attribution Theory?
3. Explain the role of social groups in Social Identity Theory.
4. What is Theory of Mind, and why is it important in childhood development?
5. How does empathy contribute to social relationships?
6. What is the purpose of the Implicit Association Test (IAT) in studying stereotypes?

Long Answer Questions

1. Discuss the process of social perception and how it influences the way we form judgments about others.
2. Explain the concept of attribution in social cognition, including the differences between internal and external attributions. Discuss how these attributions can affect social behaviour and interactions.

3. Describe the development of Theory of Mind in children, citing key experiments like the false-belief task.

4. Elaborate on how social identity theory explains the formation of self-concept and self-identity. Discuss how group memberships influence behaviour and provide examples of how this theory applies in multicultural societies.

5. Define empathy and explain its two components: cognitive empathy and emotional empathy.

6. Analyse how stereotypes, prejudices, and discrimination are related to cognitive biases, including the formation and maintenance of stereotypes.

8

Cognitive Dysfunction and Mental Health

8.1 Cognitive Disorders and Their Impact

Cognitive disorders, such as dementia, Alzheimer's disease, and attention-deficit/hyperactivity disorder (ADHD), significantly impact cognitive functions like memory, attention, and decision-making.

Cognitive disorders, including conditions like dementia, Alzheimer's disease, and attention-deficit/hyperactivity disorder (ADHD), have a profound impact on an individual's cognitive functions, such as memory, attention, and decision-making abilities. These disorders can disrupt the normal flow of daily activities, making it challenging for individuals to process information, perform everyday tasks, and engage in social interactions.

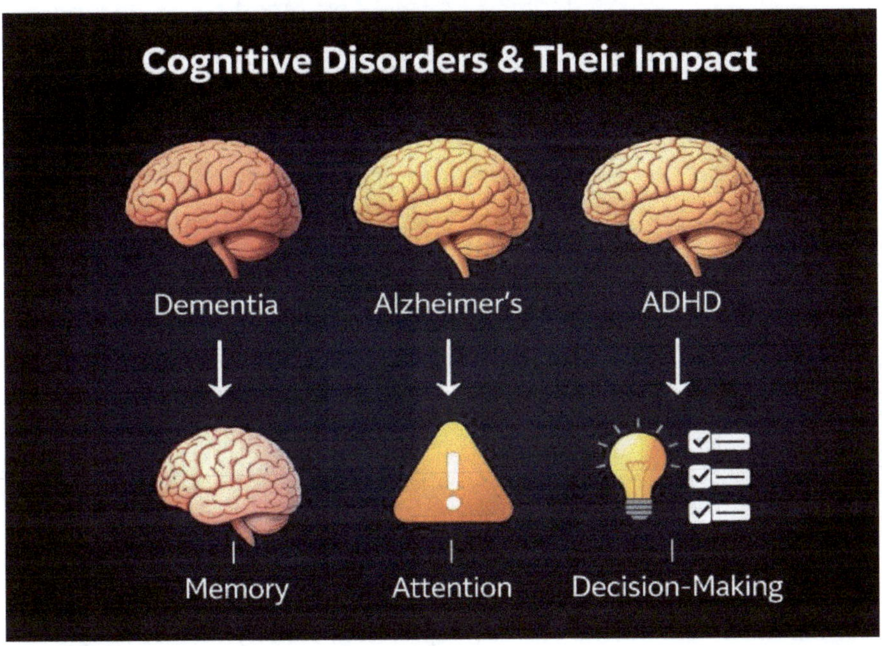

For instance, Alzheimer's disease, a progressive neurodegenerative disorder, is primarily characterized by memory loss, confusion, and difficulty in problem-solving and communication. As the disease progresses, individuals may struggle with basic tasks such as recognizing loved ones, managing personal care, and maintaining independence. In contrast, ADHD typically affects attention and impulse control, which can lead to difficulties in academic or work settings and in maintaining relationships due to distractibility and hyperactivity.

8.2 The Cognitive Aspects of Mental Health Conditions

Mental health conditions, such as depression, anxiety, and schizophrenia, often involve significant cognitive dysfunction. For example, individuals with depression may experience negative thinking patterns, which affect memory, attention, and decision-making.

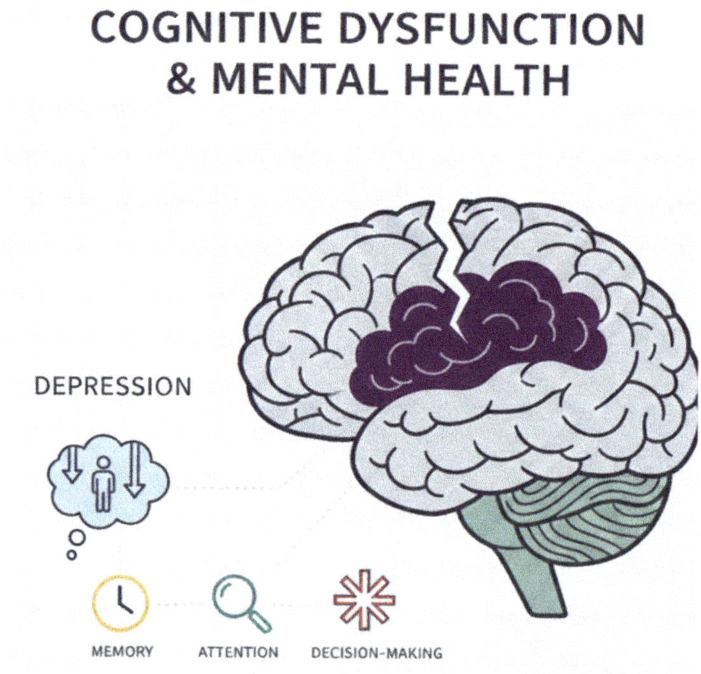

Mental health conditions such as depression, anxiety, and schizophrenia often involve significant cognitive dysfunction that affects various mental processes, including memory, attention, and decision-making. For example, individuals with depression commonly experience negative thinking patterns, which can distort their perception of reality and lead to a cycle of rumination. These cognitive distortions may manifest as pessimistic views about oneself, the future, and the world, which in turn can impair concentration and memory. Similarly, individuals with anxiety may have difficulty focusing on tasks due to constant worry, while those with schizophrenia often experience cognitive deficits in attention and working memory, making it challenging to process and respond to information.

One of the most effective treatments for these conditions is Cognitive-Behavioural Therapy (CBT), which specifically targets the cognitive aspects of mental health. CBT focuses on identifying and challenging distorted or unhelpful thought patterns that contribute to emotional distress. By helping individuals recognize the links between their thoughts, emotions, and behaviours, CBT enables them to reframe negative thinking and develop healthier, more balanced perspectives. For instance, a person with depression might be guided to recognize how their negative self-talk impacts their mood and behaviour, and to replace these thoughts with more realistic and positive alternatives.

Research has shown that CBT can significantly improve cognitive functions, such as attention, memory, and decision-making, by addressing the underlying cognitive distortions. Case studies from CBT practitioners provide real-world examples of how cognitive interventions can lead to positive changes in patients' mental well-being. These case studies demonstrate how, through structured interventions, individuals can learn to manage their emotional symptoms more effectively, leading to improved psychological health and a better quality of life.

8.3 Cognitive Therapy and Mental Health Treatment

Cognitive therapy, particularly cognitive-behavioural therapy (CBT), focuses on identifying and modifying negative thought patterns that contribute to mental health problems.

Cognitive therapy, especially Cognitive-Behavioural Therapy (CBT), is a therapeutic approach that focuses on identifying and modifying negative thought patterns that contribute to various mental health conditions. The underlying premise of CBT is that our thoughts, emotions, and behaviours are interconnected, and by changing maladaptive thoughts, individuals can alter their emotional responses and behaviours.

For instance, in depression, individuals often experience pervasive negative thoughts, such as feelings of worthlessness or hopelessness, which reinforce their low mood and lack of motivation. In anxiety, exaggerated fears and catastrophic thinking contribute to heightened stress and avoidance behaviours.

A key component of CBT is cognitive restructuring, which involves helping patients identify and confront their irrational beliefs or cognitive distortions. For example, someone with anxiety might believe, "If I don't prepare perfectly, something terrible will happen." In CBT, they would be encouraged to examine the evidence for and against this belief and to develop a more realistic, less distressing perspective. This process of cognitive restructuring is shown to improve emotional regulation, reduce stress, and increase coping skills.

8.4 Cognitive Rehabilitation

Cognitive rehabilitation is a therapeutic approach aimed at helping individuals recover cognitive functions lost due to brain injury, stroke, or neurological conditions. This form of therapy involves structured exercises designed to improve attention, memory, and executive functions.

Cognitive rehabilitation is a therapeutic approach designed to help individuals recover cognitive functions that have been impaired due to brain injuries, strokes, or neurological conditions such as Alzheimer's disease or multiple sclerosis. This form of therapy involves structured exercises and interventions aimed at improving cognitive abilities like attention, memory, and executive functions, which are crucial for everyday functioning and decision-making.

COGNITIVE THERAPY & MENTAL HEALTH

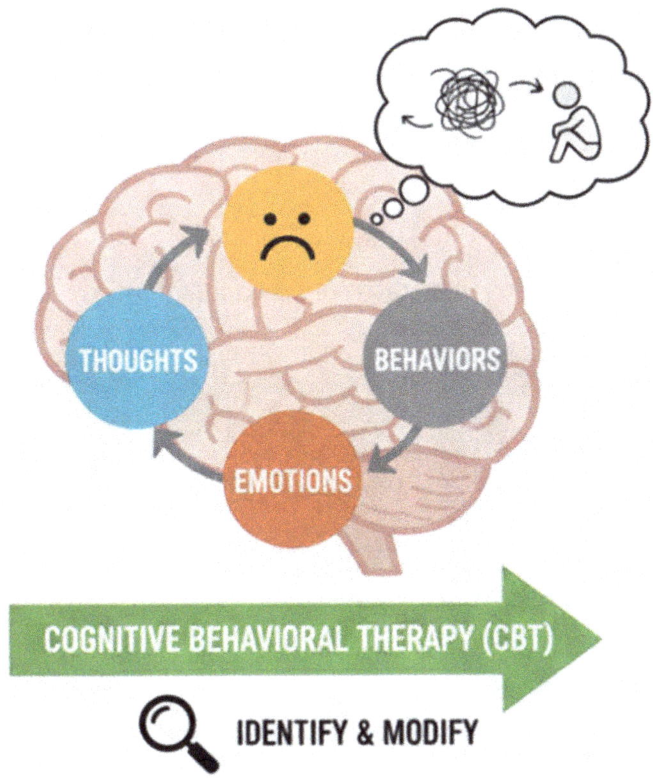

For individuals who have experienced traumatic brain injury (TBI), stroke, or other neurological impairments, cognitive rehabilitation plays a vital role in restoring lost cognitive skills. Patients may struggle with tasks such as planning, organizing, problem-solving, and remembering important details, which can significantly impact their independence and overall quality of life. Cognitive rehabilitation helps individuals relearn these skills through targeted exercises that gradually improve their cognitive abilities and enhance their functional independence.

Cognitive rehabilitation has been shown to be effective in promoting recovery and improving quality of life for individuals with cognitive impairments. Research and case studies from patients undergoing cognitive rehabilitation demonstrate its positive outcomes. Patients often report increased independence in performing daily activities, such as managing finances, cooking, and managing schedules. Long-term benefits of cognitive rehabilitation include better emotional well-being, greater confidence in one's abilities, and improved social interactions.

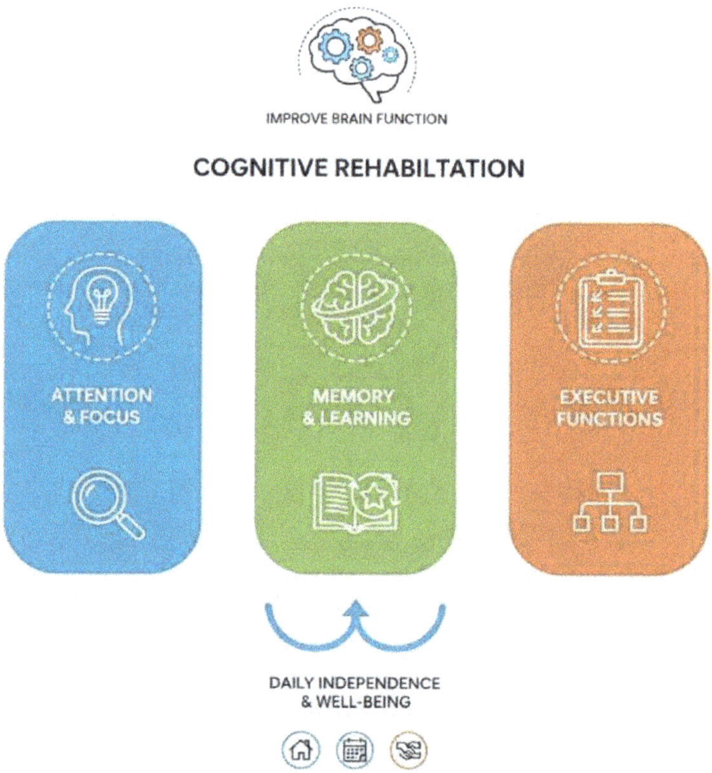

Multiple Choice Questions (MCQs)

1. Which of the following cognitive functions is most commonly impaired in individuals with Alzheimer's disease?

a) Memory
b) Visual-spatial abilities
c) Problem-solving
d) Auditory processing

Answer: a) Memory

2. Cognitive Behavioural Therapy (CBT) is most effective in treating which of the following mental health conditions?

a) Bipolar disorder
b) Schizophrenia
c) Depression and anxiety
d) Autism spectrum disorder

Answer: c) Depression and anxiety

3. Cognitive rehabilitation therapy is often used to help individuals recover cognitive functions lost due to:

a) Mental illnesses like schizophrenia
b) Brain injury or stroke
c) Genetic conditions like Down syndrome
d) Developmental disabilities

Answer: b) Brain injury or stroke

4. In Cognitive Behavioural Therapy (CBT), which of the following is a common goal?

a) Developing medications to control symptoms
b) Identifying and challenging negative thought patterns
c) Focusing on unconscious conflicts
d) Enhancing emotional intelligence

Answer: b) Identifying and challenging negative thought patterns

5. Which of the following conditions is commonly associated with cognitive dysfunction that impacts attention and executive functions?

a) Depression
b) Schizophrenia
c) Attention-Deficit/Hyperactivity Disorder (ADHD)
d) Parkinson's disease

Answer: c) Attention-Deficit/Hyperactivity Disorder (ADHD)

Short Answer Questions

1. What is the primary cognitive function impaired in Alzheimer's disease?
2. How does Cognitive Behavioural Therapy (CBT) address negative thinking patterns?
3. What role does cognitive rehabilitation play in post-stroke recovery?
4. How can cognitive dysfunction in individuals with depression affect daily life?
5. What are the key differences between cognitive dysfunction in ADHD and dementia?
6. Why is cognitive restructuring an important component of Cognitive Behavioural Therapy (CBT)?

Long Answer Questions

1. Explain the relationship between cognitive dysfunction and mental health conditions like depression and anxiety.
2. Describe the therapeutic approach of cognitive rehabilitation for individuals with traumatic brain injury (TBI). What types of cognitive functions are typically targeted during rehabilitation, and how does this therapy improve quality of life?
3. Discuss the cognitive challenges faced by individuals with post-traumatic stress disorder (PTSD). How do cognitive distortions

contribute to the emotional distress in PTSD, and what cognitive interventions are used to treat these issues?

4. Explore the impact of cognitive dysfunction on individuals with schizophrenia. How do cognitive deficits affect their ability to function in everyday life, and what therapeutic strategies can help manage these deficits?

5. How do cognitive impairments in mental health conditions like depression and schizophrenia differ from those caused by neurological disorders such as Alzheimer's disease or stroke?

6. What are the long-term benefits of cognitive rehabilitation for individuals with neurological impairments, such as stroke or brain injury?

9
The Future of Cognitive Psychology

9.1 Advances in Cognitive Neuroscience

Cognitive neuroscience is a rapidly growing field that combines cognitive psychology with neuroscience to explore the relationship between brain function and cognitive processes.

Cognitive neuroscience is an interdisciplinary field that integrates principles from cognitive psychology and neuroscience to better understand the connections between brain functions and cognitive processes. In recent years, significant advances have been made in both theoretical understanding and technological capabilities, contributing to the expansion of this field.

One of the most impactful developments has been in brain imaging techniques. Technologies like **functional magnetic resonance imaging (fMRI)** and **electroencephalography (EEG)** now allow scientists to monitor and record brain activity in real time while individuals perform various cognitive tasks. This ability to visualize the brain's inner workings has been pivotal in linking cognitive functions such as **memory**, **attention**, and **decision-making** to specific areas of the brain. For example, fMRI can identify which regions of the brain become active when a person engages in a memory retrieval task, providing insights into the neural mechanisms that underlie such processes.

Moreover, research on **neuroplasticity** has significantly altered our understanding of the brain's capabilities. Neuroplasticity refers to the brain's ability to reorganize itself by forming new neural connections in response to learning experiences, injury, or environmental changes. This phenomenon suggests that cognitive abilities are not static and can be improved over time. Targeted interventions, such as cognitive training or rehabilitation therapies, have been shown to enhance brain functions, demonstrating the potential for cognitive improvement even in adulthood or after brain injury.

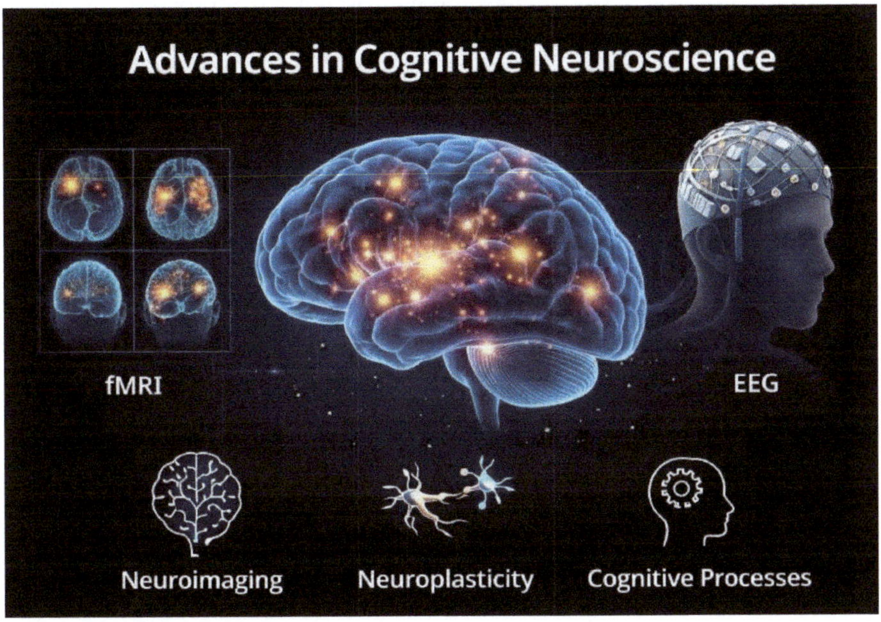

9.2 Artificial Intelligence and Cognitive Modelling

Artificial intelligence (AI) has become an essential tool in cognitive psychology, especially in the development of cognitive models that simulate human thought processes. Machine learning algorithms, which enable computers to learn from data and improve performance over time, have been used to model cognitive functions such as memory retrieval, language processing, and problem-solving.

Artificial intelligence (AI) has made significant strides in cognitive psychology, particularly in the development of **cognitive models** that aim to simulate human thought processes. By using **machine learning algorithms** , which allow computers to learn from data and enhance their performance over time, AI researchers have been able to replicate various aspects of human cognition. These advancements are crucial for both understanding the human mind and improving AI systems.

Aspect	Description
Field Definition	An interdisciplinary area combining cognitive psychology and neuroscience to study the relationship between brain function and cognitive processes.
Technological Advances	Brain imaging techniques like fMRI and EEG enable real-time monitoring of brain activity during cognitive tasks.
Key Cognitive Processes	**Memory**, **Attention**, and **Decision-making** are among the cognitive processes studied in relation to brain activity.
Neuroplasticity	The brain's ability to reorganize itself in response to learning or injury, showing that cognitive abilities can be enhanced through targeted interventions.
Impact on Treatment	Findings from cognitive neuroscience contribute to improving treatments for cognitive impairments through rehabilitation therapies and cognitive training.

Key Contributions:

1. **Memory Retrieval**: AI models simulate how humans retrieve and store memories, allowing machines to process and recall information in a way that mimics human memory systems.

2. **Language Processing**: Machine learning is used to model the human ability to understand and produce language. AI systems can analyse text or speech, predict responses, and even translate languages, closely mirroring human linguistic capabilities.

3. **Problem-Solving**: Cognitive models based on AI help simulate human problem-solving strategies. By observing patterns in human decision-making, AI can be trained to replicate these behaviours, making AI systems better at tasks such as reasoning and decision-making.

Practical Applications:

- **AI-powered chatbots** and **virtual assistants** are prime examples of AI systems that utilize cognitive models to replicate human-like interactions. These systems leverage AI to understand user input, process it, and generate appropriate responses that reflect human cognitive behaviour.

Collaborative Efforts:

Cognitive psychologists collaborate with AI researchers to build more accurate models of human cognition. These partnerships improve our theoretical understanding of cognitive processes while simultaneously enhancing the functionality of AI systems. The ultimate goal is to create AI that better mirrors human thought, improving applications across various domains, from healthcare to customer service.

9.3 The Impact of Technology on Human Cognition

Technology has profoundly affected human cognition, particularly in how we process information and interact with the world. The rise of digital tools, such as smartphones and the internet, has changed the way we access and store information.

Technology has dramatically reshaped human cognition, especially in how we process and interact with information. The proliferation of **digital tools** like **smartphones** and the **internet** has altered the way we access, store, and recall information. While these tools provide convenience and facilitate communication, they also introduce challenges that can impact cognitive functions such as **attention**, **memory**, and **problem-solving**.

Key Effects of Technology on Cognition:

1. **Information Access and Storage** : The internet allows instant access to vast amounts of information, enabling individuals to offload memory tasks and rely on digital platforms for knowledge retrieval. However, this reliance can lead to a reduction in our capacity to retain and remember information.

2. **Cognitive Overload** : With the constant availability of information, people are often faced with multiple sources of stimuli, leading to cognitive overload. This can hinder the brain's ability to focus, prioritize, and process information efficiently, resulting in shorter attention spans and difficulty concentrating on tasks for extended periods.

3. **The Google Effect** : The "Google effect" refers to the tendency for people to forget information that they know they can easily access online. Instead of committing information to memory, individuals often rely on search engines, which can diminish their ability to recall specific facts when needed. This phenomenon highlights a shift in cognitive behaviour due to the reliance on digital technology.

Cognitive Psychology's Response:

Cognitive psychologists are actively studying how these technological changes affect cognitive abilities and developing strategies to mitigate negative impacts. Key strategies include:

- **Reducing Digital Distractions** : Encouraging users to limit exposure to constant notifications and multitasking to help preserve attention span and focus.
- **Enhancing Digital Literacy** : Promoting awareness of how to effectively navigate and filter information online, helping users maintain cognitive engagement without feeling overwhelmed by the vast amount of available data.

9.4 Ethical Considerations in Cognitive Research

As cognitive psychology continues to advance, ethical issues related to research and practice become more pressing. Ethical considerations in cognitive research include issues of privacy, consent, and the potential misuse of cognitive technologies.

As cognitive psychology progresses, the rapid development of new technologies raises important ethical concerns related to both research and its application. These ethical issues must be addressed to ensure that advances in cognitive science are made responsibly and with respect for individual rights. Key ethical considerations in cognitive research include **privacy, consent**, and the potential **misuse** of cognitive technologies.

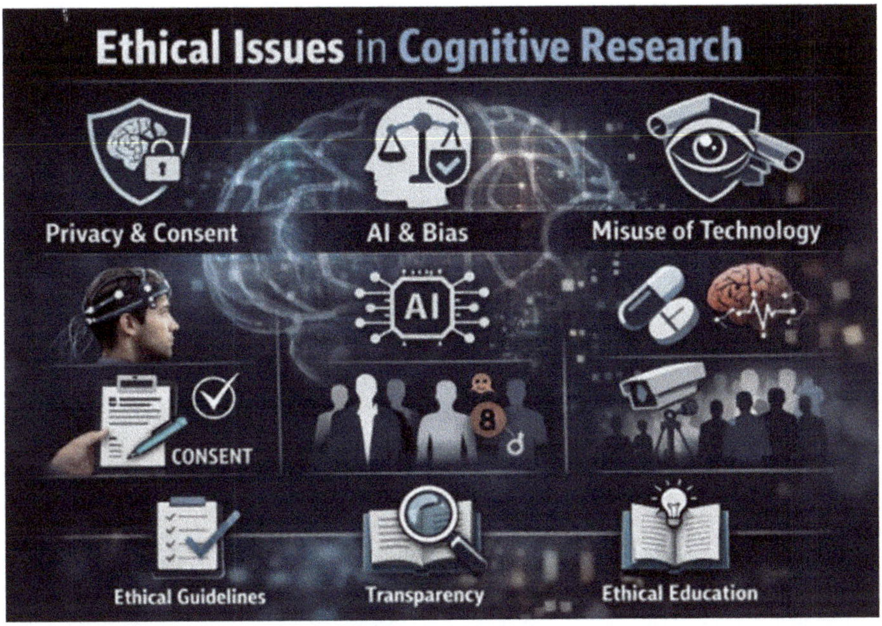

Major Ethical Issues:

1. **Privacy and Autonomy :**

Brain-Computer Interfaces (BCIs) : BCIs allow for direct communication between the brain and external devices, potentially enabling individuals to control technology through thought alone. While BCIs hold tremendous promise for individuals with disabilities, they also raise significant privacy concerns. The ability to read and influence brain activity could infringe on personal mental privacy and autonomy, potentially leading to unauthorized access to a person's thoughts or intentions.

Consent: When using advanced technologies such as BCIs or AI-based cognitive models, obtaining informed consent from participants becomes increasingly complex. Researchers must ensure that individuals fully understand the potential risks, including privacy violations and long-term impacts, before agreeing to participate in studies.

2. **AI in Cognitive Modelling :**

Bias in AI Systems: The use of AI in cognitive modelling and decision-making systems requires careful consideration of fairness and bias. AI algorithms can unintentionally reinforce biases present in the data they are trained on, leading to unfair or discriminatory outcomes. For example, decision-making systems in law enforcement or hiring practices may inadvertently perpetuate racial or gender bias if not carefully monitored.

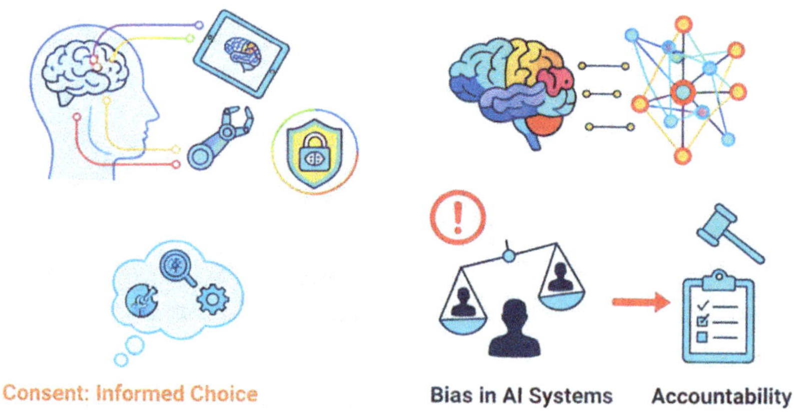

Accountability: The ethical use of AI requires clear accountability mechanisms. If AI systems make critical decisions about individuals, such as in health diagnoses or legal judgments, determining responsibility for those decisions-especially if an error occurs-becomes a pressing ethical challenge.

3. **Misuse of Cognitive Technologies :**

Cognitive Enhancement: While technologies that enhance cognitive abilities, such as neurostimulation or nootropic drugs, may have therapeutic benefits, their misuse for non-medical enhancement poses ethical dilemmas. For instance, there may be concerns about social inequality if such technologies become available only to certain groups, further deepening cognitive disparities.

Surveillance: Advances in cognitive technologies, including facial recognition and emotion detection, can be misused for surveillance and control, raising questions about the balance between security and individual freedoms.

Ethical Issue	Description
Privacy and Autonomy	Concerns about the potential for cognitive technologies, like Brain-Computer Interfaces (BCIs), to infringe on mental privacy and autonomy by accessing or influencing brain activity.
Informed Consent	The complexity of obtaining informed consent for studies using advanced cognitive technologies, ensuring participants fully understand potential risks and impacts.
Bias in AI Systems	The risk that AI algorithms used in cognitive modelling and decision-making systems may reinforce existing biases, leading to unfair or discriminatory outcomes.
Accountability in AI Decisions	The need for clear accountability in cases where AI makes important decisions (e.g., in healthcare, legal systems) to ensure responsibility for errors or harm.
Misuse of Cognitive Enhancement	Ethical concerns over the use of cognitive technologies, such as neurostimulation or nootropic drugs, for non-medical enhancement, potentially leading to inequality.
Surveillance	The potential misuse of cognitive technologies like emotion detection and facial recognition for surveillance purposes, impacting individual freedoms.

Navigating Ethical Dilemmas:

Cognitive psychologists and researchers must carefully navigate these ethical challenges while continuing to explore and expand our understanding of the human mind. Some key steps to mitigate ethical concerns include:

- **Establishing Ethical Guidelines** : Research institutions and policymakers should develop comprehensive ethical guidelines for the use of cognitive technologies, ensuring that privacy, consent, and fairness are upheld.
- **Transparency and Accountability** : Researchers and AI developers must prioritize transparency in how cognitive technologies are designed, deployed, and tested, allowing for greater public trust and accountability.

Ongoing Ethical Education : Cognitive psychologists and technologists must engage in continuous education about ethical practices and emerging issues, ensuring they are equipped to handle new challenges as technology evolves.

Multiple Choice Questions (MCQs)

1. What is one of the primary challenges in the future development of cognitive psychology?

A) Developing more advanced brain-computer interfaces
B) Ensuring the ethical application of AI in cognitive modelling
C) Reducing the cost of cognitive research
D) Improving computational power for simulations

Answer: B) Ensuring the ethical application of AI in cognitive modelling

2. How is the integration of artificial intelligence (AI) expected to influence cognitive psychology?

A) By eliminating the need for human cognitive models
B) By providing tools to simulate and understand complex cognitive processes
C) By making cognitive psychology obsolete
D) By focusing solely on memory enhancement

Answer: B) By providing tools to simulate and understand complex cognitive processes

3. Which area of cognitive psychology is most likely to benefit from advancements in neuroplasticity research?

A) Memory and learning processes
B) Social cognition
C) Decision-making strategies
D) Visual perception

Answer: A) Memory and learning processes

4. What role does brain-computer interface (BCI) technology play in the future of cognitive psychology?

A) It will replace traditional cognitive psychology methods entirely
B) It will enable direct interaction between human cognition and external devices
C) It will primarily focus on enhancing human emotion regulation
D) It will be used to develop new cognitive disorders

Answer: B) It will enable direct interaction between human cognition and external devices

5. In the future of cognitive psychology, which ethical concern is expected to grow in significance?

A) The environmental impact of cognitive research
B) The privacy of brain data and personal mental processes
C) The financial cost of cognitive technologies
D) The need for more rigorous statistical analysis in research

Answer: B) The privacy of brain data and personal mental processes

Short Answer Questions

1. What role will artificial intelligence play in the future of cognitive psychology?

2. How might advancements in neuroplasticity influence cognitive therapy?

3. What are the ethical concerns surrounding brain-computer interfaces (BCIs)?

4. How could cognitive psychology benefit from improved brain imaging techniques?

5. What is the potential impact of cognitive psychology on enhancing learning in educational settings?

6. Why is the study of cognitive models important for the development of AI systems?

Long Answer Questions

1. Explain how the integration of artificial intelligence with cognitive psychology can enhance our understanding of human cognition.

2. Discuss the potential ethical dilemmas that may arise with the use of brain-computer interfaces in cognitive research and daily life. How can these issues be addressed in future research?

3. Describe the implications of neuroplasticity research for cognitive rehabilitation therapies.

4. How do emerging technologies in cognitive psychology, such as neuroimaging and BCIs, provide new avenues for studying complex cognitive processes like attention, memory, and decision-making?

5. Analyse the future of cognitive psychology in education. How can cognitive psychology's understanding of memory, learning, and problem-solving be applied to develop better teaching methods and tools?

6. In what ways can cognitive psychology contribute to the development of ethical AI systems?

References

Chapter 1: The Foundations of Human Cognition

1. Neisser, U. (1967). *Cognitive Psychology*. Appleton-Century-Crofts.
2. Miller, G. A. (1956). The magical number seven, plus or minus two: Some limits on our capacity for processing information. *Psychological Review*, 63(2), 81-97. https://doi.org/10.1037/h0043158
3. Baddeley, A. (2000). *The episodic buffer: A new component of working memory?* Trends in Cognitive Sciences, 4(11), 417-423. https://doi.org/10.1016/S1364-6613(00)01538-2

Chapter 2: Memory and Learning: The Cognitive Architecture

1. Atkinson, R. C., & Shiffrin, R. M. (1968). Human memory: A proposed system and its control processes. In K. W. Spence & J. T. Spence (Eds.), *The psychology of learning and motivation* (Vol. 2, pp. 47-89). Academic Press.
2. Baddeley, A., & Hitch, G. J. (1974). Working memory. In G. H. Bower (Ed.), *The psychology of learning and motivation* (Vol. 8, pp. 47-89). Academic Press.
3. Ebbinghaus, H. (1885). *Memory: A Contribution to Experimental Psychology*. Dover Publications.

Chapter 3: Perception: The Lens Through Which We See the World

1. Gibson, J. J. (1979). *The Ecological Approach to Visual Perception*. Houghton Mifflin.
2. Gregory, R. L. (1997). *Perception as a cognitive process*. In D. G. M. Hart & H. T. Rees (Eds.), *Perception: An essay on the philosophy of perception* (pp. 17-46). Oxford University Press.
3. Rock, I. (1983). *The Logic of Perception*. MIT Press.

Chapter 4: Decision-Making and Problem-Solving

1. Kahneman, D., Slovic, P., & Tversky, A. (1982). *Judgment under Uncertainty: Heuristics and Biases*. Cambridge University Press.

2. Simon, H. A. (1955). A behavioural model of rational choice. *Quarterly Journal of Economics*, 69(1), 99-118. https://doi.org/10.2307/1884852

3. Gigerenzer, G., & Todd, P. M. (1999). *Simple Heuristics that Make Us Smart*. Oxford University Press.

Chapter 5: The Role of Emotion in Cognition

1. Lazarus, R. S. (1991). *Emotion and Adaptation*. Oxford University Press.

2. Damasio, A. R. (1994). *Descartes' Error: Emotion, Reason, and the Human Brain*. Grosset/Putnam.

3. Goleman, D. (1995). *Emotional Intelligence: Why It Can Matter More Than IQ*. Bantam.

Chapter 6: Cognitive Development Across the Lifespan

1. Piaget, J. (1952). *The Origins of Intelligence in Children*. International Universities Press.

2. Vygotsky, L. S. (1978). *Mind in Society: The Development of Higher Psychological Processes*. Harvard University Press.

3. Erikson, E. H. (1950). *Childhood and Society*. Norton & Company.

Chapter 7: Social Cognition: Understanding Others and Ourselves

1. Fiske, S. T., & Taylor, S. E. (2017). *Social Cognition: From Brains to Culture* (3rd ed.). SAGE Publications.

2. Heider, F. (1958). *The Psychology of Interpersonal Relations*. John Wiley & Sons.

3. Tajfel, H. (1974). *Social Identity and Intergroup Relations*. Cambridge University Press.

Chapter 8: Cognitive Dysfunction and Mental Health

1. Berrios, G. E. (1996). *The History of Mental Symptoms: Descriptive Psychopathology since the Nineteenth Century*. Cambridge University Press.

2. Beck, A. T. (1976). *Cognitive Therapy and the Emotional Disorders*. International Universities Press.

3. Kramer, J. H., & Boone, K. B. (2009). Neuropsychological assessment of dementia. *Journal of Clinical and Experimental Neuropsychology*, 31(5), 429-436. https://doi.org/10.1080/13803390802242077

Chapter 9: The Future of Cognitive Psychology

1. Raichle, M. E. (2015). The Brain's Default Mode Network. *Annual Review of Neuroscience*, 38, 433-447. https://doi.org/10.1146/annurev-neuro-071013-014030

2. Clark, A. (2015). *Surfing Uncertainty: Prediction, Action, and the Embodied Mind*. Oxford University Press.

3. Marr, D. (1982). *Vision: A Computational Investigation into the Human Representation and Processing of Visual Information*. W.H. Freeman.

Appendix

1. Glossary of Key Terms

1. **Cognitive Psychology**: The branch of psychology that studies mental processes such as perception, memory, reasoning, problem-solving, and decision-making.
2. **Working Memory**: A system for temporarily storing and manipulating information required for cognitive tasks such as reasoning, learning, and comprehension.
3. **Neuroplasticity**: The brain's ability to reorganize itself by forming new neural connections throughout life.
4. **Attribution Theory**: A theory that explains how people infer the causes of their own and others' behaviours, attributing them either to internal factors (e.g., personality) or external factors (e.g., environment).
5. **Cognitive Bias**: Systematic patterns of deviation from norm or rationality in judgment, whereby inferences about other people and situations may be drawn in an illogical fashion.
6. **Heuristics**: Mental shortcuts or rules of thumb that simplify decision-making, often leading to faster but sometimes biased conclusions.
7. **Theory of Mind (ToM)**: The ability to attribute mental states-such as beliefs, intents, desires, emotions, and knowledge-to oneself and others.
8. **Cognitive Dissonance**: The psychological discomfort experienced when holding two or more contradictory beliefs, values, or attitudes.
9. **Implicit Association**: Unconscious associations between concepts (e.g., race and traits) that influence attitudes and behaviour.

10. **Social Identity**: The part of an individual's self-concept derived from their membership in social groups.

2. Data Sources and Datasets

1. **Cognitive Neuroscience Database**: A database containing data on brain activity linked to various cognitive tasks, obtained using neuroimaging techniques like fMRI and EEG.
2. **Human Connectome Project**: A large-scale initiative that maps the human brain's neural connections, providing valuable data on the brain's structure and function.
3. **Psychological Research Databases**: Platforms like PsycINFO and PubMed provide access to thousands of peer-reviewed journals, articles, and studies on cognition and psychology.
4. **Implicit Association Test (IAT)**: A widely used dataset for studying implicit biases, available at Project Implicit (https://implicit.harvard.edu).
5. **National Institutes of Health (NIH) Cognitive and Neurocognitive Data**: The NIH provides data on cognitive health, aging, and mental health conditions that can be analysed for patterns in cognition.
6. **Open Science Framework**: A platform for sharing data sets related to cognitive psychology experiments and studies, including open-source datasets on memory, attention, and problem-solving.

3. Tools and Frameworks

1. **SPSS (Statistical Package for the Social Sciences)**: A software used for statistical analysis in cognitive psychology research, useful for data processing, hypothesis testing, and reporting findings.
2. **MATLAB**: Widely used in cognitive neuroscience for processing complex data, particularly from neuroimaging and brain-computer interface (BCI) studies.

3. **E-Prime**: A software for creating and running psychological experiments, particularly in areas like attention, perception, and memory.
4. **Psychtoolbox**: A set of MATLAB tools designed for running behavioural experiments in cognitive psychology, particularly those involving visual stimuli.
5. **fMRI Analysis Software**: Tools like FSL and SPM (Statistical Parametric Mapping) are commonly used for analysing neuroimaging data and understanding the neural underpinnings of cognition.
6. **R**: A programming language and environment for statistical computing, often used for data analysis and visualization in cognitive psychology research.

4. References for Further Reading

1. Anderson, J. R. (2005). *Cognitive Psychology and its Implications* (6th ed.). Worth Publishers.
2. Gazzaniga, M. S., Ivry, R., & Mangun, G. R. (2018). *Cognitive Neuroscience: The Biology of the Mind* (5th ed.). W.W. Norton & Company.
3. Eysenck, M. W., & Keane, M. T. (2015). *Cognitive Psychology: A Student's Handbook* (7th ed.). Psychology Press.
4. Baddeley, A. (2000). *The Episodic Buffer: A New Component of Working Memory?* Trends in Cognitive Sciences, 4(11), 417-423.
5. Kahneman, D. (2011). *Thinking, Fast and Slow*. Farrar, Straus and Giroux.
6. Vygotsky, L. S. (1978). *Mind in Society: The Development of Higher Psychological Processes*. Harvard University Press.

7. Clark, A. (2015). *Surfing Uncertainty: Prediction, Action, and the Embodied Mind*. Oxford University Press.

8. Damasio, A. R. (1994). *Descartes' Error: Emotion, Reason, and the Human Brain*. Grosset/Putnam.

5. Future Directions in Cognitive Psychology

1. **Integration of AI and Cognitive Modelling** : Future research will focus on using artificial intelligence (AI) to create more sophisticated models of human cognition, allowing for deeper insights into the cognitive processes that drive behaviour. AI tools will also aid in the development of cognitive neuroproteins, improving cognitive functioning for individuals with cognitive disorders.

2. **Neuroplasticity and Lifelong Learning** : The ongoing study of neuroplasticity will open new possibilities for understanding how the brain adapts throughout life, particularly in aging adults. Research will explore how cognitive skills can be enhanced through training and learning interventions.

3. **Cross-Cultural Cognitive Psychology** : There is a growing interest in understanding how cultural differences shape cognitive processes. Future studies will examine how various cultural contexts affect memory, decision-making, and problem-solving, leading to a more globally nuanced understanding of cognition.

4. **Digital Age and Cognitive Overload** : With the rise of digital technologies, cognitive psychology will increasingly focus on how constant information bombardment affects attention and memory. Research will aim to identify strategies to mitigate cognitive overload in the digital era, balancing the benefits and drawbacks of technological advancements.

5. **Emotional and Cognitive Integration** : Future research will delve deeper into how emotion and cognition are interwoven, particularly

how emotional regulation affects cognitive processes like decision-making, memory retrieval, and problem-solving.

6. Summary of Key Points

- **Cognitive psychology** studies mental processes like perception, memory, and problem-solving, focusing on how people acquire, process, and store information.
- **Memory** involves different processes, including encoding, consolidation, and retrieval, which can be enhanced using techniques like mnemonic devices and spaced repetition.
- **Perception** is shaped not only by sensory input but also by cultural and experiential factors, and cognitive illusions highlight the limitations of our perceptual systems.
- **Decision-making** and **problem-solving** are influenced by heuristics and cognitive biases, while cognitive styles dictate individual approaches to solving problems and making decisions.
- **Emotion** and **cognition** are deeply connected, with emotions shaping cognitive processes, while emotional intelligence plays a vital role in interpersonal and decision-making skills.
- **Cognitive development** progresses through stages, from childhood learning to adult problem-solving, and declines with aging, although some cognitive functions remain stable.
- **Social cognition** explores how individuals understand themselves and others, while stereotypes and prejudices can distort social judgments, impacting relationships and behaviour.
- **Cognitive dysfunction** occurs in mental health disorders like depression and schizophrenia, and cognitive therapies, such as CBT, are used to address these dysfunctions.

ABOUT THE AUTHOR

Dr. Anu Kant Mital is an eminent psychiatrist, academic, and global mental health consultant with over three decades of experience in clinical psychiatry and psychological sciences. A graduate of Grant Medical College, Mumbai, he holds an M.D. in Psychiatry, a Ph.D. in Psychology from MAG H University (UK), and an M.A. in Psychology. His extensive training spans clinical hypnotherapy, family therapy (UK), criminology, and biomedical ethics. Dr. Mital has served as a UNESCO Unit Head in Biomedical Ethics (Haifa) and as an External Consultant with the United Nations CISMU. He is currently a Consultant Psychiatrist at several prestigious institutions including Jupiter Hospital, Masina Hospital, and Godbole Heart Hospital. He has held academic leadership roles such as Dean at FIAMC Biomedical Ethics Centre and in the past as the Professor of Psychiatry at R.G. Medical College. His international exposure includes service within the UK NHS and observation at the University of Berne, Switzerland.

10. E-LIBRAIRIE – France (French online bookstore)
11. Everand – India (Everand Book Distributor is based in India)
12. EXLIBRIS – Switzerland
13. Fable – United Kingdom (UK/Europe digital subscription book service)
14. Flipkart – India
15. GANDHI.com – Mexico (Librerías Gandhi)
16. Google Book – United States (Google LLC)
17. Google Audio Book – United States (Google LLC)
18. IBS.IT – Italy Wikipedia
19. Indigo – Canada
20. Kobo – Canada Wikipedia
21. Kindle – United States (Amazon product)
22. LAFELTRINELLI – Italy Wikipedia
23. Lehmanns – Germany
24. Lulu – United States
25. MORAWA – Austria
26. Rakuten Japan – Japan (Rakuten)
27. Smashwords – United States
28. Tolino / Thalia – Germany (Tolino is a German-language eBook ecosystem, Thalia DE)

29. Vivlio – France
30. Saxo – Denmark (Saxo.com)
31. YES24 – South Korea

and others.

🎁 You will receive 20 physical author copies FREE to your Indian address.

⭐ You can also receive 5 book reviews:

* 3 reviews by eminent university professors

* 2 reviews from your own group/colleagues/seniors/teachers

www.books.wissira.us

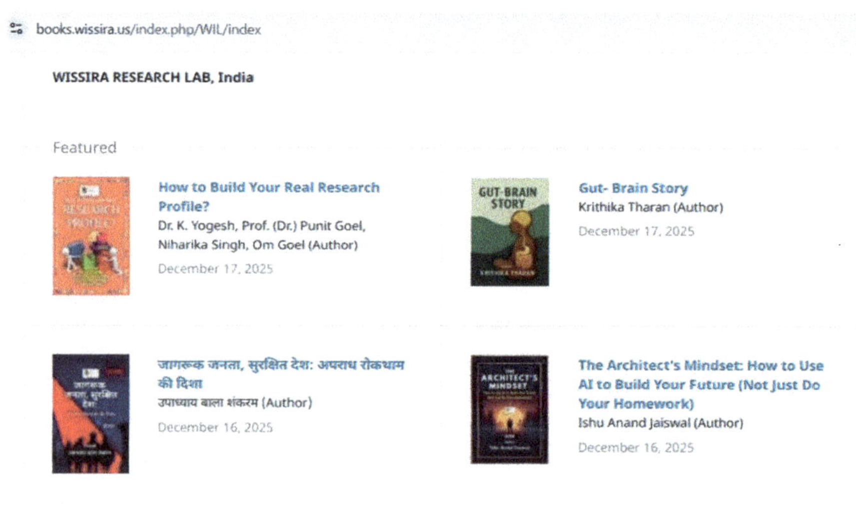

www.books.wissira.us

DOI: https://doi.org/10.63345/book.wrl.2512000324

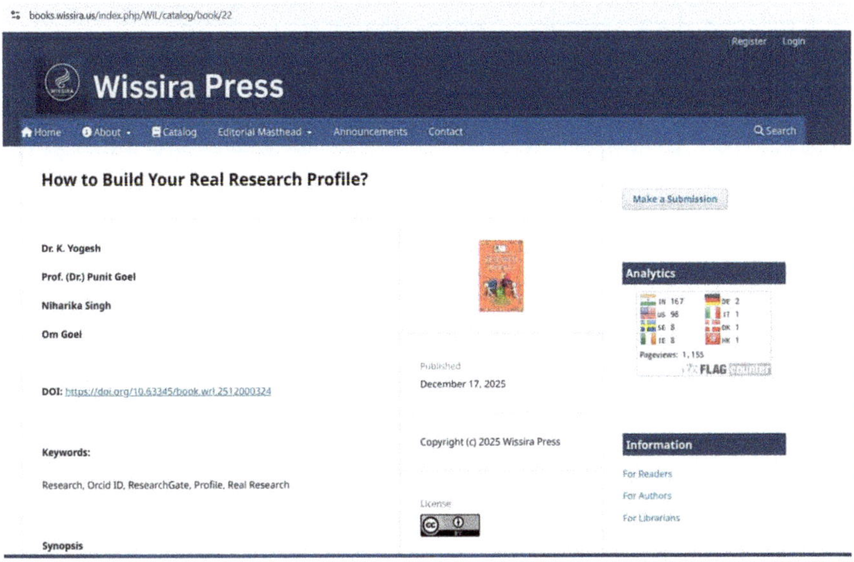

https://books.wissira.us/index.php/WIL/login

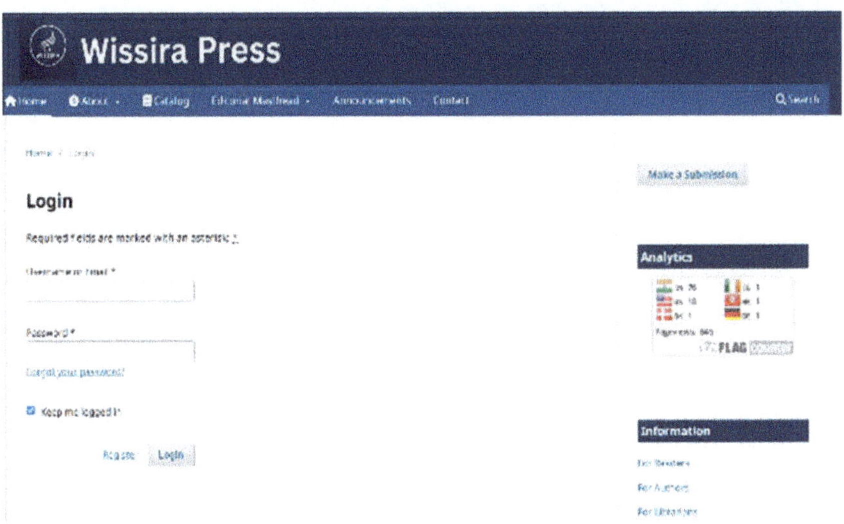

https://books.wissira.us/index.php/WIL/catalog

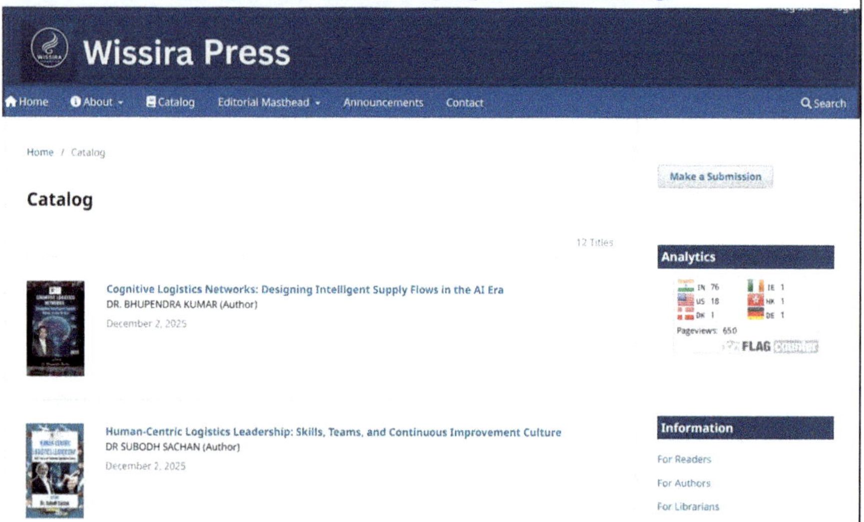

https://books.wissira.us/index.php/WIL/about/contact

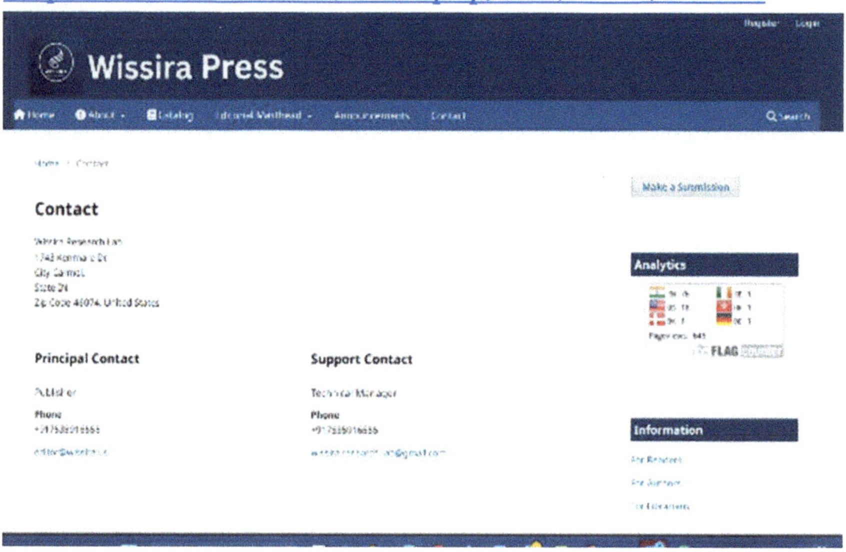

https://www.amazon.in/dp/B0G7MQFD2L

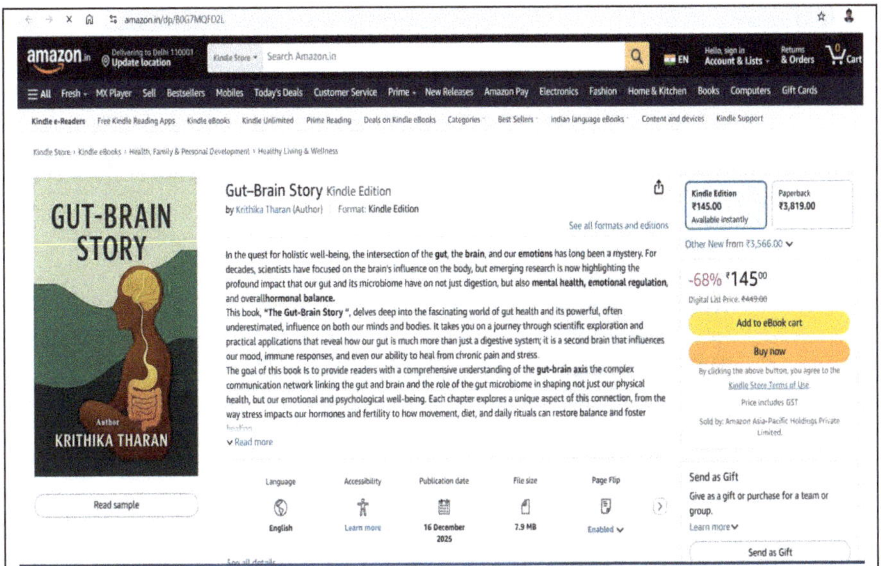

https://books.apple.com/us/book/the-architects-mindset-how-to-use-ai-to-build-your/id6756545876

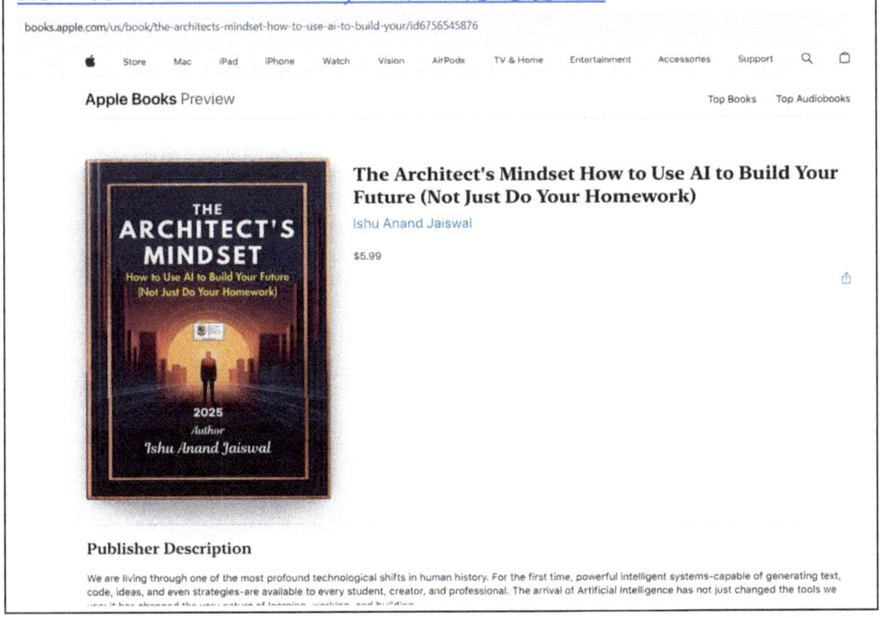

Flipkart:
https://tinyurl.com/WissieaPressBook250306Human

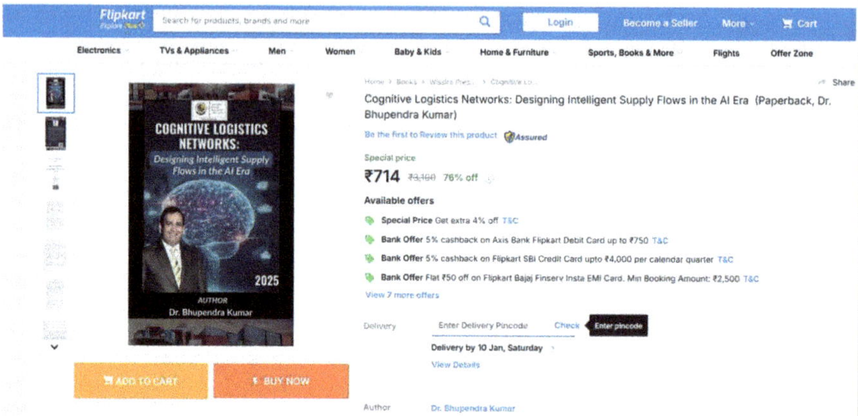

https://play.google.com/store/audiobooks/details?id=AQAAAEAa9DeoPM

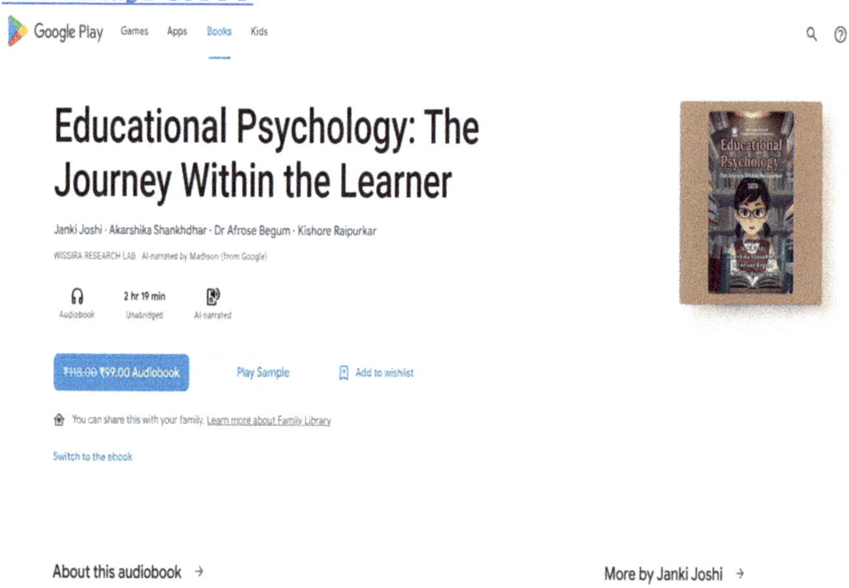

https://shop.vivlio.com/product/9798232547615_9798232547615_10020/human-centric-logistics-leadership-skills-teams-and-continuous-improvement-culture

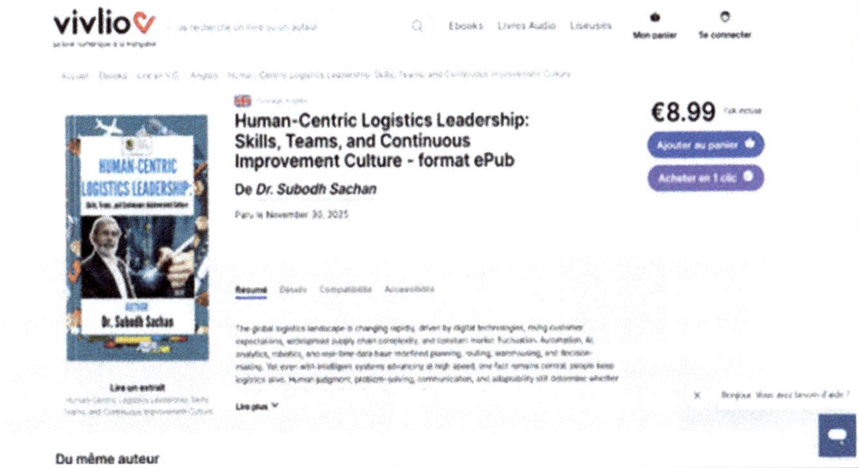

https://www.kobo.com/in/en/ebook/from-shakespeare-to-tagore-reinterpreting-english-literature-through-indian-sensibility?sId=070486d4-8aef-4220-a1d2-26bb2ba8ecb6&ssId=3FJLsnB4eTMdnS31kaTcM

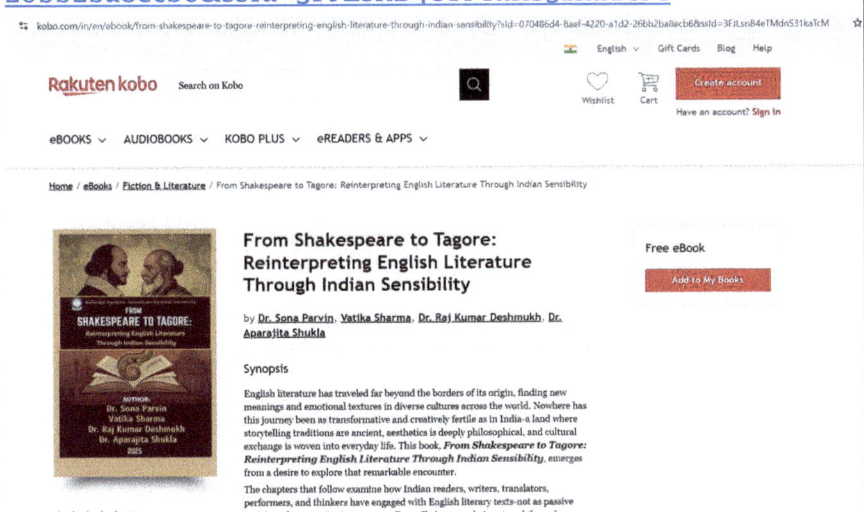

https://fable.co/book/x-9798230804772

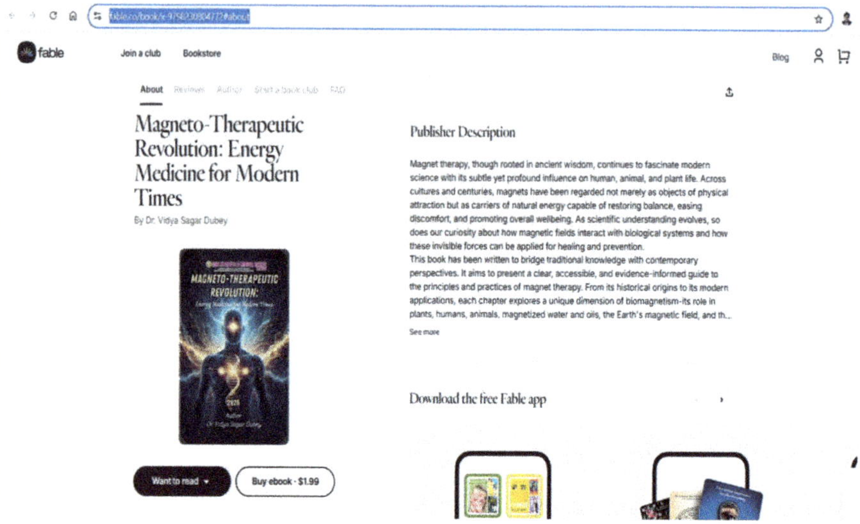

https://www.lulu.com/shop/dr-subodh-sachan/human-centric-logistics-leadership/ebook/product-rmj4erq.html?q=Human-Centric+Logistics+Leadership%3A+Skills%2C+Teams%2C+and+Continuous+Improvement+Culture&page=1&pageSize=

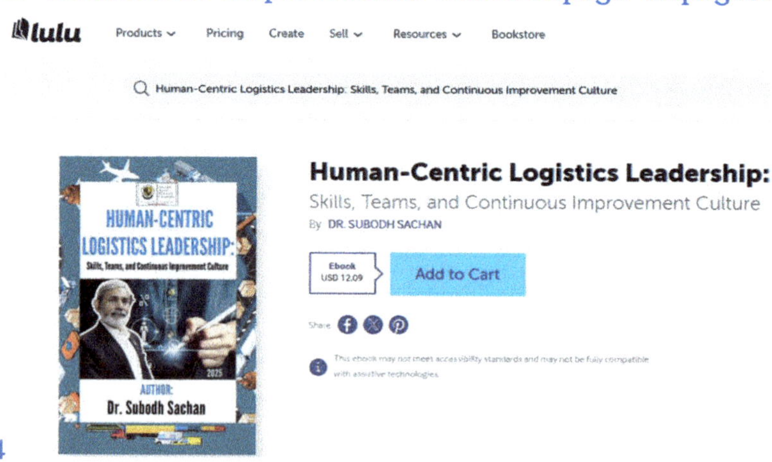

4

https://play.google.com/store/audiobooks/details?id=AQAAAEDqoRHh6M

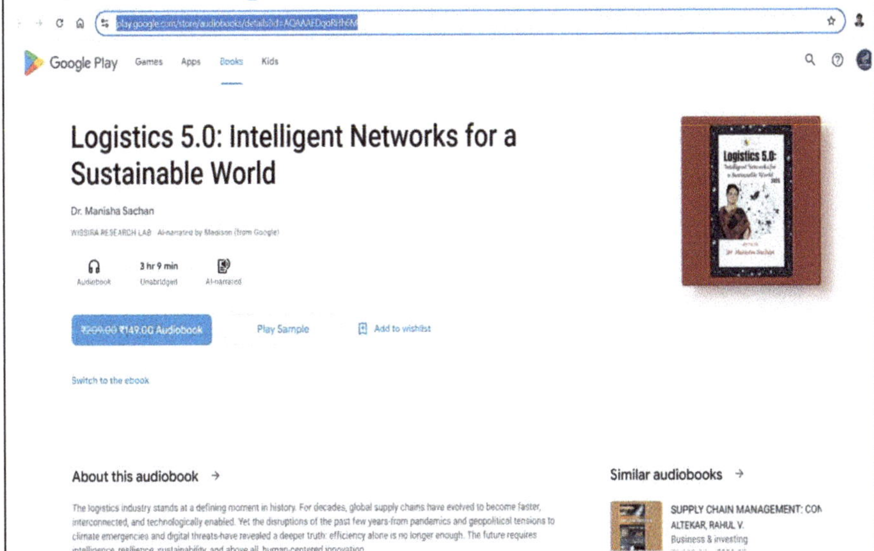

https://play.google.com/store/books/details?id=TbmfEQAAQBAJ

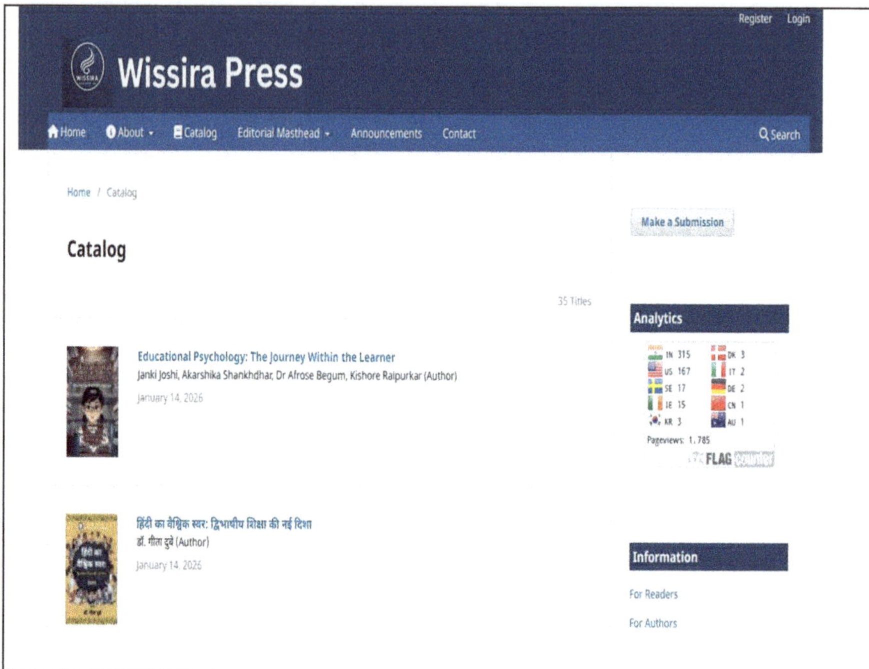

https://www.smashwords.com/books/view/1943936

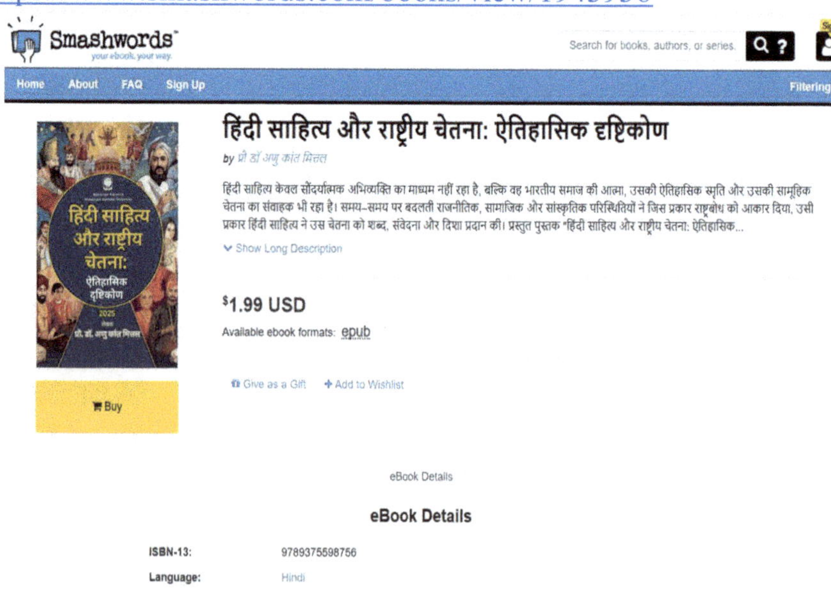

Analytics

IN	135	IT	1
US	84	DK	1
SE	8	HK	1
IE	8	DE	1

Pageviews: 1,012

FLAG counter

Amazon Kindle

Amazon

Flipkart

LULU

Apple Books

Barnes & Nobles

Everand

Fable

Kobo

Information

For Readers

For Authors

For Librarians

Keywords

sustain long-term operational excellence.

Across the nine chapters of this work, readers will find a structured and practical approach to understanding how leadership influences logistics outcomes. Beginning with the foundations of human-centric leadership, the book explores essential competencies such as communication, empathy, decision-making, and ethical responsibility-skills that enable leaders to build credibility and trust in high-pressure environments. It then moves deeper into the dynamics of teamwork, motivation, and empowerment, highlighting how resilient and collaborative teams become the backbone of

Smashwords

Tolino

Vivlio

Google Books

---

www.ingramcontent.com/pod-product-compliance
Ingram Content Group UK Ltd.
Pitfield, Milton Keynes, MK11 3LW, UK
UKHW021411190726
13845UKWH00028B/1017

9 789375 598374